THE CLASSIC & CRAFT COCKTAIL RECIPE BOOK

THE
CLASSIC
& CRAFT
COCKTAIL
RECIPE BOOK

Clair McLafferty

ROCKRIDGE
PRESS

This book is dedicated to my dear husband, and the countless bartenders who have answered my questions and made me feel at home.

CONTENTS

FOREWORD

Clair McLafferty has finally written the book I wanted to find when I moved to San Francisco in the summer of 2000. I'd just left an office job in New Mexico and moved to the West Coast intent on getting a job as a bartender, despite never having actually bartended. I figured: *I'm 24, I'm able-bodied, there are hundreds of bars and restaurants in San Francisco, I'm familiar with the use of hand towels, how hard can it be?*

As it turns out hard, really hard.

It took me about a month (and the kind advice of the 68th restaurant manager I interviewed with) to figure out I needed some relevant experience on my resume. After I started getting auditions (they actually called them auditions) based on fictitious experience, it quickly became apparent that I didn't know what I was doing. I needed information—fast!

So I bought books. All the bartending books I could find at San Francisco's grandest bookstores were grossly deficient. They were either old lists of drinks with recipes measured in gills or "wineglasses," giant encyclopedic tomes on wine, or poorly written bartending memoirs with advice like "Read the sports page. Have at least 5 jokes ready to go. Wipe the bar often. Keep a small bat handy."

I did what I could. I made 3x5-inch flash cards of cocktails, types of wine, and jokes. I memorized 50 drinks nobody had ordered in 50 years ("Income Tax Cocktail," anyone?) and a pocketful of jokes to try out on unsuspecting co-workers. I put on a tie, ironed my apron, had an anxiety attack *(they're gonna know I don't know anything!)* and went to an audition at a fancy-ish restaurant downtown, where a nice lady at the bar smiled at me and ordered a Cosmopolitan. I froze. That wasn't one of the flash cards. So I smiled back, wiped the spotless bar in front of her, and told her a joke. So much for bartending books in the year 2000. Somehow I made it through that shift, outsourcing that Cosmo and many, many other drinks to the wildly competent woman I was working with, while doing a lot of wiping.

During the thousands of shifts since then, I have learned, through trial and error, about tools, techniques, spirits, liqueurs, cocktails, beer, wine, etc. You know—all the stuff explained in this book you hold in your hands. You have it so easy! All you need to do is turn the page and you'll already have a considerable advantage.

Now there are more good bartending books than ever. Which one to pick? Start here in Clair's capable hands, you won't be disappointed. She does the Herculean job of explaining the basics in plain language while filtering out the superfluous and irrelevant. Clair, where were you in 2000 when I needed you so desperately?!

But seriously, Clair, thank you for writing such a clear and concise guide to drinks. To the wildly competent woman who looked after me during that first audition, thank you for picking up the slack and not telling anyone I didn't have a clue. And Mom, thank you for taking me aside at Thanksgiving and teaching me how to make a Cosmo.

Jon Santer
Owner of Prizefighter
Emeryville, California

INTRODUCTION

This comprehensive bar guide is not only a primer on making cocktails; it is also a love letter to them. It may sound cheesy, but a few years ago, cocktails changed the course of my life. At the time I was working at my third dead-end office job, and I hated it. To cope with the office politics and stress, I frequented a neighborhood cocktail bar. Every night I went, I tried new cocktails and asked the bartenders question after question. Each new bit of information revealed a new world of things I did not know. It was, pardon the pun, intoxicating. One night, after a couple of drinks, I asked the bar manager when he was going to stop telling me about cocktails and start teaching me how to make them.

A couple of weeks later, I started as a barback. I quit my office job soon after. Six weeks later, I was bartending solo. My new job gave me an excuse to learn everything about cocktails, spirits, and drinking culture. I spent all my free time practicing technique, memorizing recipes, and reading cocktail books. But I quickly reached the boundaries of what they could teach and began digging into my own historical research. Soon, I was arguing good-naturedly with customers about the correct Sazerac recipe—in my dreams. (According to my husband, I was sleep talking about the Sazerac formula.)

Through it all, my favorite part of bartending was sharing what I had learned. As a bartender and writer in the relatively new craft cocktail scene in Birmingham, Alabama, I found numerous opportunities. Many people had encountered these drinks elsewhere and were excited to have them here, but just as many thought craft cocktails were pretentious and stuck to their usual orders. Little by little, the joy of sussing out the exact cocktail a new guest would love grew.

Making craft cocktails accessible to everyone started opening doors. Behind the bar, I could practice my explanations for cocktails and spirits and tweak them so they were concise, witty, and accurate. Watching customers' faces light up after discovering they liked something they had previously avoided was absolutely priceless. Soon after,

I could turn around and use the descriptions in articles and, later, in classes.

In 2015, I left my full-time bar position to write. Since then, I have covered everything from the contentious science of aging whiskey and the craft bitters boom to common injuries behind the bar. But I miss the camaraderie of working behind the bar, of tasting new products and tweaking new cocktail recipes. I miss the regulars who became friends, but most of all, I miss watching new customers realize that craft cocktails are awesome.

This book is what I wish I could have studied when I started bartending. It covers just about everything behind the bar and gives what I hope are practical tips for developing your own technique to mix drinks. Experiment, and do not be afraid to take chances or make mistakes in mixing drinks. Even if it is not exactly to your taste, you will still end up with a drink in hand.

HOW TO USE THIS BOOK

This book begins with "The Bar" and "The Art" (pages 15 and 51), chapters on the basics of building a bar and the art of making good use of it. Here, you will find a catalog of equipment and bar tools, glassware, and almost every drink ingredient imaginable, plus recipes for making your own infusions, bitters, syrups, and garnishes. Next, "The Craft" (page 59) shows what sets craft cocktails apart from others and how to create your own. Part 2, "The Recipes" (page 69), provides formulas for classic standards and modern craft cocktail recipes. These recipes are organized by their base ingredient: champagne and sparkling wine, gin, rum, vodka, and so on, plus there are a few fun chapters that cover drinks for a crowd ("Punches," page 267), and instant parties ("Shooters," page 277).

The cocktails in these pages are some of the most iconic from the last 200 or so years, but we have also included some of the most recognizable dive-bar classics. Despite its serious beginnings, the craft cocktail movement has taken many of the dive-bar classics and remade

INTRODUCTION

them with craft ingredients to bring some playfulness and fun back to bartending. I am not ashamed to say I have made some damn fine White Russians (page 192) or that I love Lüft Bar's Zima (page 202).

Many of the recipes in this book may vary by region. Wisconsin natives will tell you that both Old Fashioned recipes (page 219) are wrong because they call for whiskey and lack lemon-lime soda. Others will tell you that the proportions of some drinks are off. When you mix cocktails at home, you will invariably find some too sweet, too bitter, or too strong. That is okay—no two people like exactly the same things. I have included one or two general tasting notes with each recipe to help direct your exploration. And, luckily, there are ways to tweak your already-made cocktails to make them perfectly suit your taste (see page 62 under "Craft Your Own").

You will find no chapter dedicated to liqueurs in this book; instead, their cocktail recipes are grouped in with their base spirits. If a recipe is not where you think it ought to be, check the drink recipe index in the back; it may be located in another alcohol's chapter. Also, champagne, which is a type of wine, is used in craft cocktails more than any other, so it gets its own chapter. Other wines, fortified wines, and beers are combined into one chapter, because they usually appear as cocktail modifiers rather than base ingredients.

I have included modern recipes from some of the world's most recognizable craft bartenders including Jim Meehan, Kate Gerwin, Colin Shearn, and Beckaly Franks—these are marked with a bowtie symbol (>◁). The indexes at the back of this book will help keep all these recipes at your fingertips; flip to the recipe index (page 312) to find a cocktail by name, or search the general index (page 317) for anything from a favorite mixer to a specific type of garnish.

For current and aspiring bartenders of any profession, I hope this book will be a handy resource as well as a springboard into crafting your own cocktails.

PART ONE

The Essentials

CHAPTER ONE

THE BAR

Equipment and Bar Tools

There is no other way to say it: Well-designed bar tools are sexy. Today they are available in a variety of food-safe finishes, which allows you to customize the look of your bar equipment.

Wading through catalog page after catalog page of beautiful utensils can make stocking a fully functional bar seem prohibitively expensive. Luckily, many of the extravagant gadgets that combine two (or three, or four) tools into one are not necessary. Some people may exclaim that a bar is not truly complete without a silver ice bucket and matching scoop or perfectly personalized bar spoon, but only a few tools are absolutely necessary to make most drinks.

This book groups tools into three categories: essential, advanced, and optional. This designation will hopefully help you determine how important the tools are to the craft. Before you get overwhelmed at the number of "essentials," take a second to step back. Quite a few of these are also staples of a well-equipped kitchen and do not have to be specially designated as barware. Plan to build up the other, more specialized tools over time.

Even the most seasoned bartender is sometimes caught without equipment. For those times, some entries here include an "In a pinch" note describing common household items that can be substituted for bar tools if absolutely necessary.

ESSENTIAL BAR TOOLS

Bar spoon: This tall utensil is useful when stirring drinks, grabbing garnishes like maraschino cherries and olives, and measuring small quantities of ingredients. Unlike a tableware spoon, it is designed to move easily in confined areas like tall glasses, mixing glasses, and jars. **In a pinch:** *Use a regular spoon from your silverware drawer.*

Bottle opener: A bottle opener removes metal bottle caps from bottles. The simpler the better—the basic model's two sides, a rounded cutout and a circular opening, can be used to remove bottle caps and wrest stuck pour spouts, respectively.

In a pinch: *At your own risk, Google how to use a lighter or the edge of a countertop as a bottle opener. But for the love, refrain from using your teeth.*

Champagne stoppers: These spring-loaded stoppers are designed to fit tightly around the neck of a bottle to preserve carbonation in champagne or other sparkling wines. Look for those with a rubber washer on the rounded end to help seal the bottle.

Citrus juicer, handheld: A handheld device that extracts juice from citrus fruits. These come in a variety of sizes to accommodate different fruits. Look for one that can fit oranges, as most other citrus fruits will fit as well. Some bartenders believe these are more efficient than industrial citrus juicers.

In a pinch: *Halve the citrus and squeeze with your hand.*

Cocktail shakers: Shakers come in many shapes and sizes. Although cobbler shakers with built-in strainers are the most widely available, they do not seal well and may leak if shaken vigorously. Most bartenders prefer a Boston shaker (an 18-ounce metal tin and a 12-ounce pint glass) or a Parisian shaker (one 18-ounce and one 28-ounce metal tin).

Corkscrew: Corkscrews come in many shapes, sizes, and prices. The main differences among the different types, including the centuries-old T-shaped design, electric push-button models, and lever pull corkscrews, mainly boil down to control. Most of these are easily inserted into the cork, but many provide too much or too little torque for removing it. Too much, and the cork gets shredded, but too little and the cork stays where it is. The best are the small, cheap, portable tools often used by servers. These usually have a corkscrew coil, bottle opener, and a knife for removing foil from the bottle neck.

Cutting board: A sturdy cutting board makes a great surface for preparing fruit, herbs, garnishes, and other cocktail ingredients.

Hawthorne strainer: This strainer, also known as a cocktail strainer, has a spring coil around its edge that allows it to fit snugly

THE BAR

over the edge of a cocktail shaker to hold back ice, fruit, and other unwanted solids.

In a pinch: *Use a whisk to cover the mouth of the shaker.*

Ice cube tray: Ice cube trays come in all materials, shapes, and sizes. Start with a silicone tray of 1-inch cubes. Larger pieces will come in handy for stirred drinks you want to keep cool without a lot of dilution. If you want to drink straight, chilled spirits without any dilution, invest in whiskey stones that can be cooled in the freezer.

Jigger: Although a jigger traditionally refers to a 1½-ounce measurement, the standard pour for most classics is 2 ounces. Here, the jigger refers to the tool we use to measure out liquid ingredients in cocktails. Look for a double-headed one that has a 2-ounce measure and a 1-ounce measure.

Knife: A sharp paring knife is ideal for cutting garnishes and halving citrus for juicing. You can use a larger knife if that is all you have.

Liquid measuring cups: Larger measuring devices are crucial for making syrups and measuring other liquids in large quantities.

Measuring spoons: Some recipes call for a teaspoon or less of a certain ingredient. Keep a partial set of measuring spoons on hand just in case.

Mixing glass: Though a cut-glass Yarai mixing glass is a gorgeous addition to any bar, a pint glass or mason jar will suffice. Some older cocktail books may call for martini pitchers with glass stirring rods instead of mixing glasses with bar spoons, but they are similar enough that separate equipment is not necessary. If you use a pint glass, gently hold the base while stirring to minimize the chance of spillage.

Muddler: A muddler is the ideal tool for crushing fruit or bruising herbs to release their juices or natural oils. Look for one with a good grip. If you are considering a wooden muddler, buy one made from untreated wood.

In a pinch: *Use the handle of a wooden spoon.*

ADVANCED BAR TOOLS

Blender: For frozen drinks, the ideal blender has a powerful enough motor to crush ice and purée fruit without leaving chunks or lumps behind. Although a blender is not strictly essential, it is fun to have.

Fine strainer: Fine strainers are typically used to remove pulp, tiny ice shards, and other small particulates from cocktails. While juicing, they can also be used to strain pulp out of citrus juice to slightly extend its shelf life.

Julep strainer: Mainly used for straining stirred drinks, this strainer holds back larger pieces of ice while allowing smaller pieces of mint or other herbs into the cocktail, making it ideal for juleps or cobblers.

Lewis bag and mallet: For drinks like the Mint Julep (page 218) that require crushed ice, a canvas Lewis bag and either a rolling pin or mallet are the cheapest alternative to a shaved ice machine. These canvas bags wick water away from the ice and were staples of 1800s bars that were repopularized in the 1990s by the Lewis Corporation. **In a pinch:** *Place ice in a plastic bag wrapped in a bar towel and smash with a hammer.*

Pour spouts: These spouts help you control the flow of liquor or liqueur out of a bottle, helping keep measurements accurate and cocktails consistent.

OPTIONAL BAR TOOLS

Absinthe fountain: Despite their name, absinthe fountains are used to dispense water, not absinthe. These ornate vessels allow drinkers to control the flow of water over sugar cubes into their glasses of absinthe.

Absinthe spoon: These trowel-shaped spoons are perforated or slotted so they can hold a sugar cube while the absinthe fountain drips ice-cold water onto it, slowly dissolving it into a glass of absinthe.

THE BAR

Citrus juicer, press or electric: If a hand juicer becomes painful or is inadequate, spending the extra money on a larger citrus press or electric juicer can save prep time—and hand cramps.

Decanter: These containers are used for decorating a bar and aerating wines or whiskies. Decanters make even bottom-shelf liquors look good, but their contents should be drunk quickly. Antique leaded crystal decanters are still readily available, but for storing alcohol long-term, decanters may not be your best option. They are better used for parties and special occasions.

Ice bucket and scoop: Your freezer will work just fine for holding your ice, but an ice bucket and scoop can add sophistication to your bar. If you use a metal set, place a towel or mat beneath it to prevent condensation from forming and potentially damaging your bar.

Swizzle sticks: These individual drink stirrers (and garnish grabbers) come in many shapes and sizes. They can also help mix a drink by acting as a sort of whisk that is rubbed between the hands to rotate. Material-wise, swizzle sticks range from colorful plastic tiki tools to real wood.

Know Your Glassware

Today you can find glassware in an almost infinite number of designs, colors, shapes, and purported functionalities. To help you begin to sort through the multitude, this section explains the glassware that is named in the cocktail recipes that follow.

Because this is a practical guide, we have grouped the glassware into three categories: essential, advanced, and optional. Though having a wide range of serving vessels available gives your bar a certain *je ne sais quoi*, it is absolutely not necessary.

That said, in drinking, presentation plays a key role in determining whether you will enjoy a beverage. Drinks served in beautiful glassware or bottles are often perceived as being of higher quality, a phenomenon known within the industry as "drinking the label." Although it is unclear whether the glassware makes a measurable scientific difference in taste, it does impact the experience.

On a more practical level, some glasses do what they are designed to do. These vessels keep a hot drink hot, enhance the aromatics of a Cognac or wine, or even preserve some of the carbonation in a sparkling wine.

The illustrations that accompany each drink are the most recognizable versions of these glasses. Further, the capacity listed with each glass is the ideal for use with cocktails. To make sure your drinks stay cold, chill the glasses unless the cocktail is served over ice.

As previously stated, although this list is rather hefty, not every piece is absolutely essential. Realistically, to start making cocktails, use whatever you have on hand. When you start building your home bar, you really need only six or eight of each type of glass.

ESSENTIAL GLASSWARE

Champagne flute: This is the preferred glass for champagne and sparkling wines. This tall, narrow glass helps prevent bubbles from dissipating. These flutes hold 6 to 9 ounces on average and are also perfect for cocktails made with champagne.

Collins glass: *Collins* and *highball* are often used interchangeably, though Collins glasses tend to be a bit narrower. They hold 10 to 12 ounces. The 10-ounce version will work for most fizzy cocktails served over ice.

Coupe glass: Best known for its role in wedding champagne toasts, this 3- to 5-ounce glass's wide mouth makes it less than ideal for retaining carbonation. It is much better suited for serving classics like the Daiquiri (page 151), and in a pinch it can be used instead of a cocktail glass.

THE BAR

Heatproof mug: A 10-ounce heatproof mug is perfect for everything from a Hot Toddy (page 300) to an Irish Coffee (page 300). Although more specialized glasses like the Irish coffee mug may be beautiful and appealing, mugs tend to be more versatile and wider-mouthed, allowing ethanol fumes to evaporate.

Pint glass: Though many beer lovers argue that the 16-ounce pint glass damages a beer's taste and aroma, it is handy to have around for backyard barbeques and beers that are better served cold. They can also be used as mixing glasses.

Rocks glass: Also called a lowball glass, old fashioned glass, or tumbler, the rocks glass typically holds between 4 and 8 ounces. It is handy for serving everything from straight pours of whiskey to Old Fashioneds (page 219) to drinks served on the rocks, such as Scotch and sodas.

Shot glass: These hardy little glasses typically hold about 1½ ounces. Though they can be used like a rudimentary jigger for proportional measurements, they are more commonly used for shots or shooters.

Wineglass, red: If you are only looking to buy one type of wineglass, most bartenders will suggest these. Typically, these 14- to 24-ounce stemmed glasses have a wider mouth designed to allow wines to release their aromas. They are also often used for Sangria (page 274), sangaree, and highball drinks, especially the Gin and Tonic (page 117).

ADVANCED GLASSWARE

Cocktail glass: This is traditionally similar to a martini glass, but with a more rounded bowl. In most cases the two can be used interchangeably, though do note that martini glasses tend to be larger. However, as with a martini glass,

THE CLASSIC & CRAFT COCKTAIL RECIPE BOOK

those that are more conical are not well balanced. Most cocktails will fit in a 5½-ounce cocktail glass.

Double rocks glass: Also known as a double old fashioned glass, these typically hold between 12 and 16 ounces.

Julep cup: Traditionally, the 12-ounce julep cup is silver or silver plated and used to make the Mint Julep (page 218), the official drink of the Kentucky Derby, and other juleps, such as the Prescription Julep and the Champagne Julep (same page).

Martini glass: See cocktail glass.

Mule mug: This 16-ounce copper mug is perfect for keeping the Moscow Mule (page 194) and its many variations frosty.

Pilsner glass: This tall, V-shaped glass is designed to show off the color of light beer and to preserve its carbonation. It usually holds 12 to 16 ounces.

Spirits glass: A tulip-shaped spirits glass typically holds around 5 ounces but is used for 1½- or 2-ounce straight pours of spirits sampled at room temperature.

OPTIONAL GLASSWARE

Cordial glass: Like a more elegant shot glass with a stem, this is typically used for after-dinner liqueurs.

Fizz glass: Usually holding about 8 ounces, the straight-sided fizz glass is designed for soda-topped drinks made with or without an eggy component.

Hurricane glass: This 20-ounce glass is typically used for Hurricanes (page 152) but can also be used for other juice-heavy tipples.

Margarita glass: A variation on a coupe glass, the margarita glass is used for the frozen and iced versions of the cocktail in the United States. But this glass is not necessary for drinking a margarita, especially if you would prefer not to spend the money on one-use glassware.

 Punch cup: Traditionally found as part of a punch bowl set, the punch cup typically resembles a teacup. These rounded crystal cups often have handles and hold 6 to 8 ounces.

 Snifter: Traditionally used for sipping brown spirits, such as brandy and fine Cognac, snifters range from 5 to 25 ounces and are thought to enhance the spirit's aromatics.

 Sour glass: Sour glasses are used for sours of all kinds and some crustas. Also known as a Delmonico or whiskey sour glass, this short-stemmed glass typically holds 5 or 6 ounces.

 Tiki mug: Although originally created as a marketing tool for tropical tiki cocktails, this festive mug is usually used to serve traditional tiki cocktails like the Mai Tai (page 161) or the Zombie (page 166). The tipples inside are often as fearsome as the mugs' visages, but significantly more delicious, and they range anywhere from 12 to 32 ounces.

 Wineglass, white: The typical white wine glass often has a narrower bowl than its red counterpart to keep the wine chilled for longer. These are also sometimes used to serve iced mixed drinks.

Liquid Gold: Stocking the Bar

Keeping up with the ever-growing number of cocktail ingredients can be difficult, even for professional bartenders. Despite the variety, some ingredients that have been used for more than a century can be hard to find in stores. To add to the confusion, some ingredients popular in far-flung corners of the world have made their way into common markets—with or without clearly labeled packaging. This diversity has added a huge range of new flavors to cocktail palates but can make it difficult to tease out what constitutes the basics of a cocktail.

Traditionally, cocktails and liqueurs are made with one of the following six liquors: brandy, gin, rum, tequila, vodka, and whiskey. Liqueurs are also essential to cocktail-making; these sweet beverages range from creamy and savory to fruity and light to bitter and herbal. Additional liquids that belong behind every bar include wines, beers, sodas, syrups, and bitters. What follows is a bartender's glossary.

LIQUORS

Many of the most recognizable alcohols in the world are classed as liquor: Gin, rum, tequila, vodka, and whiskey are all in that category. But thanks to the craft cocktail boom, they are joined by others like absinthe, cachaça, and mezcal. If a bad reputation precedes any of these spirits, do not believe it: Much of their exotic or bad boy appeal is based on misinformation. For example, absinthe has been legal in the United States for about a decade, and it will not make you hallucinate—it never did.

What, exactly, defines a liquor? As it turns out, it is a rather fluid matter, pun intended. Most experts separate liquor from beer and wine as having been distilled from a fermented mixture of grain, sugar, milk, agave, or something else. The process of distillation separates the water and alcohol, usually with either heat or cold. But what they are distilled from and how they are distilled determines what they are called. Though distillation was originally a tool for making medicines and remained such for centuries, it is now definitively in the world of recreational drinking.

You will probably notice that liquor accounts for at least half of most classic cocktails. A moderately priced, midrange quality liquor will work for almost all of these. Do skip the bottom shelf: Spending just a few dollars more will exponentially increase the quality of your drinks—and possibly save you the pain of a hangover.

Note that most premium spirits are not designed to be mixed and will not work as well in mixed drinks or cocktails. That is not to say that using top-shelf liquor in drinks is verboten, but rather that it is not necessarily advisable.

For most classic cocktails, except the Cosmopolitan (page 193), steer clear of flavored liquor. Its sugar content is often higher than that of the plain spirit, which will change the flavor profile of the cocktail—and not always for the better.

LIQUEURS

Though most liqueurs are based on distilled spirits, there are some differences between the two. Liqueurs tend to be higher proof, and most have sugar added. Though flavored vodkas and rums are classed as liquors, their sugar content probably places them closer to liqueur status than anything else. Some of the categories are more like unofficial delineations based on the liqueur's main flavor. These include *amari*, bitter Italian liqueurs often drunk with espresso; fruit liqueurs; cream liqueurs; crème liqueurs, which have lots of sugar added and a syrupy texture; and coffee liqueurs.

This class of booze fits into the drinking world in a rather unique way. Though some are imbibed in place of dessert, others are designated as pre- or post-dinner drinks, and still others are used mainly as ingredients in cocktails. The following liqueurs are included here because they are frequently used in classic cocktails. You may notice that absinthe is not on this list. Although it is used as a seasoning in many drinks, absinthe traditionally does not have any sugar added.

Amaretto: This liqueur has an almond flavor, as it is made from apricot kernel oil or almond oil, depending on the producer.

Anisette: This anise-flavored liqueur is commonly consumed in Mediterranean countries. Though similar to a pastis, anisette tends to be lower in alcohol content.

Aperol: This light, citrusy, bittersweet liqueur is a very mild amaro.

B&B: As a mixture of brandy and Bénédictine, B&B is quite similar to the cocktail of the same name: spicy and fairly dry.

Baileys cream liqueur: Based on Irish whiskey, cream, and a proprietary blend of spices, Baileys is the world's best-selling cream liqueur. It is most frequently used in hot drinks and shots.

Bärenjäger: This German liqueur is honey flavored and vodka based.

Bénédictine: This mysterious, brandy-based liqueur is purported to have been created by the Bénédictine monks as a health elixir. According to the company, only three people know the recipe at any time.

Campari: This is the most famous amaro. Though originally using cochineal for coloring, the recipe was changed in 2006 to use a dye that would not fade over time. This extremely bitter aperitif is used most famously in the Negroni (page 119), though it is also wonderful with soda.

Chambord: This brandy-based sweet black raspberry liqueur is made in France.

Chartreuse: As the story goes, Carthusian monks created this herbal liqueur. The green, which is made from at least 130 botanicals, and yellow, which is lighter and sweeter, as well as long-aged V.E.P. versions of each color are available in the United States. The premium version, Chartreuse Elixir Végétal, is thought to be made from the original seventeenth-century recipe.

Cointreau: This well-known brand of brandy-based Triple Sec is flavored with dried orange peels.

Crème liqueurs: Interestingly enough, crème liqueurs do not contain dairy. Instead, they are heavily sweetened and often high-proof liqueurs made from a variety of ingredients.

- Crème de cacao: chocolate
- Crème de café: coffee
- Crème de cassis: black currant
- Crème de menthe: peppermint
- Crème de pêche: peach
- Crème de violette: violets

Curaçao: From the Caribbean island of Curaçao, this liqueur is made from sour orange peels. It is colorless, but some varieties are tinted blue with food colorant.

Cynar: This artichoke-based Italian liqueur is flavored with thirteen herbs and plants. For an amaro, it is relatively mild.

Drambuie: This Scotch-based, honey-sweetened herbal liqueur is produced in Edinburgh.

Fernet Branca: Love it or hate it, the slight minty, bitter black liqueur is drunk before dinner to stimulate the appetite and afterward to aid in digestion.

Frangelico: A popular Italian hazelnut liqueur, Frangelico is flavored with cocoa, vanilla, and other plants and tinted with caramel coloring.

Galliano: A sweet herbal liqueur used both as a digestif and a cocktail ingredient, Galliano is most commonly used in the Harvey Wallbanger (page 195).

Godiva: With added bitter orange, this rich chocolate liqueur comes in a white chocolate version as well.

Grand Marnier: A popular orange-flavored liqueur created in the nineteenth century, this brandy-based drink is flavored with distilled bitter orange peel.

Heering: Popular in Denmark, this blood-red liqueur is flavored with Danish cherries and a spice blend.

Jägermeister: Since its creation in 1878, Jäger has been made from a blend of 56 herbs and spices. It is often drunk as a chilled shot or an unchilled digestif or used in cocktails.

Kahlúa: A coffee-flavored, rum-based liqueur from Mexico.

Kümmel: A sweet, clear liqueur flavored with cumin, caraway seed, and other herbs and spices.

Limoncello: This lemon-flavored liqueur is mainly produced in Southern Italy.

Maraschino: This cherry liqueur is made from sour marasca cherries. It tends to be more dry than sweet, and some brands like Maraschino use the whole fruit, which gives it a nutty flavor.

Midori: A bright green melon-flavored liqueur produced by spirits behemoth Suntory.

Nocello: Produced in Italy, Nocello is a walnut- and hazelnut-flavored liquor.

Parfait d'Amour: With a name like *perfect love*, it is not surprising that purple liqueur is similar to crème de violette, but it has more of a citrusy note. In Europe it is Curaçao-based and delicate, while the American version is much heavier on the citrus.

Pastis: This term describes a group of clear, strong, anise-flavored liqueurs. Like absinthe, they will cloud when water is added.

Pernod: Often used as an absinthe substitute, Pernod is a pastis with heavy anise flavor.

Pimm's No. 1: This gin-based herbal British liqueur is used most notably in a Pimm's Cup (page 134). Though five other Pimm's liqueurs were produced for a time, the No. 1 is the only one still produced year-round.

Rock and rye: A citrusy, rye whiskey–based liqueur flavored with a variety of fruits.

RumChata: This rum-based cream liqueur is flavored to be like an alcoholic horchata, which in Latin American countries and Spain is a popular and refreshing milky-looking drink made of ground nuts, seeds, or rice and spices.

Sambuca: This licorice-flavored Italian liqueur is similar to anisette but is usually served with a garnish of three coffee beans.

Sloe gin: A gin-based liqueur made with blackthorn berries, which are nicknamed sloe berries.

Strega: Named for the Italian word for *witch*, Strega is an herbal Italian liqueur hailing from Benevento.

Tia Maria: A Jamaica rum–based coffee liqueur.

Triple Sec: This orange liqueur is similar to Curaçao but likely originated in France as an answer to Curaçao.

Underberg: A pungent, bitter herbal liqueur from Germany. Like many other liqueurs, Underberg is made from a proprietary formula, so the true contents are unknown.

Unicum: A bittersweet herbal liqueur from Hungary made in Vienna.

WINE

Most cocktail bars have a wine list, but wines are included in this book solely for their role in proto-cocktails. Before bartenders or home drinkers were whipping up afternoon tipples with distilled spirits, they were likely mixing and buying wine already mixed with spices and sometimes sugar. Though these additions were often to mask the taste of subpar hooch, they also taught our forefathers how to experiment with the flavors of alcoholic beverages.

Wine is a type of alcoholic beverage made from fermenting fruit juice, usually grapes. Thanks to archaeologists, we know that humans have been drinking wine since at least the Neolithic period, or 8500 to 4000 BCE. Some scientists believe that humans may have been drinking fermented fruit juice as far back as the Stone Age. Back then, the fruit or juice fermented naturally as yeast in the air interacted with the fruit.

Though some winemakers still use this process, called *spontaneous fermentation*, the results are unpredictable. Along with the type of grapes, the yeast strain deeply influences the final taste of the wine. It makes sense that many winemakers and brandy producers have proprietary yeast strains. But possibly the most desirable flavors come from how the grape is produced. This flavor profile, called the *terroir*, differs with every location, as it reflects the land where the grapes are grown.

Fortified wines are a bit more complicated. In these, a grape-based spirit is added to bump up the alcohol content. Some, like vermouths and quinas, are spiced and flavored with different herbs and plants. In the days before refrigeration, it is likely that these products were more convenient for bartenders, as they would not spoil. As a result, they, especially sherry, are found in more cocktail recipes than table wines are.

BEERS

These alcoholic beverages are made by fermenting grain. Most beers are made with malted barley. Like wine, it has been drunk for much longer than distilled spirits. Once distillation was introduced, beer was distilled into whiskey. In ancient Egypt, as well as in many other cultures, a low-alcohol beer was a dietary staple. Then, in the 1400s, the Dutch began flavoring beer with hops. The resulting beer changed drinking history: Hops acted as both a flavoring agent and a preservative, making beer slightly more shelf stable and more portable. It also added even more variety to available beers, leading to the rainbow of selections we enjoy today.

INFUSIONS

Finding flavored liquor that is not chock-full of sugar or artificial flavors is extremely difficult. Luckily, infusions are a relatively quick way to ensure that your liquor does not taste like chemicals or candy. It is no wonder, then, that the technique behind them has been used for centuries to preserve spices and herbs and improve the taste of subpar alcohol. Once all the ingredients are together, all it takes is time.

A neutral spirit like vodka may seem like the easiest place to start, but do not write off other spirits. Infusing rum, tequila, and whiskey with complementary flavors can make a good drink great. To make sure you do not waste your booze, start out by experimenting with flavors that are often used in cocktails made with that spirit. Whiskey goes well with cinnamon, apples, coffee, and other harvest flavors, while rum infuses well with everything from coffee and vanilla to tropical fruits.

For best results, start with high-quality spirits, fruits, and herbs. Keep a glass container on hand that holds at least 1½ liters and has an airtight lid, along with several cheesecloths, coffee filters, and a funnel. Do not throw out the original bottle—you can strain the infusion back into it for easier storage and pouring.

How long you will leave the ingredients to steep depends on the flavors you are using. Herbs like mint or basil turn bitter if steeped too long. Heartier flavors like raspberry and pineapple may take a couple of weeks, but strong citrus flavors will shape up in a day or two. Unsweetened infusions should keep up to about a year at room temperature, unless the recipe mentions otherwise, but if you are concerned about it, keep it in the fridge. If it gets to the point where it tastes funky or not quite right, toss it.

RUM INFUSION RECIPES

Each type of rum (page 143) will pair well with different flavors. Light rum can be the base for just about anything, whereas darker rum can best be highlighted with vanilla, caramel, or tropical fruit. Many of the rum infusions at bars are the tropical, fruity variety, but those flavors do not have to define it. Fruity flavors like pineapple add an extra layer to classics like the Daiquiri, but rum is versatile enough that it can also be paired with coffee, cocoa, and other dark flavors. If you would prefer, substitute vodka or another liquor for rum in any of the following recipes.

Pineapple Rum MAKES 1 (750-ML) BOTTLE
KNIFE, SEALABLE LARGE GLASS JAR, FINE STRAINER, FUNNEL

1 fresh, ripe pineapple
1 to 2 (750-ml) bottles light or dark rum

Wash the pineapple, and cut off the top and bottom. Core the fruit, but leave the rind on, and slice the flesh into large chunks. In a sealable large glass jar, cover the pineapple chunks with the rum. Seal and let sit at room temperature (out of direct sunlight or extreme cold) for at least 1 week, shaking every day or two. Taste the rum. If the flavor is not strong enough, let sit for another week, shaking every couple of days. Once the flavor is to your taste, remove the pineapple chunks. Strain the rum through a fine strainer, funnel back into the original bottle or bottles, and label.

If you like Piña Coladas: *Pineapple rum goes well in pretty much any rum drink or in a rum-based Sazerac. If you are feeling adventurous, keep the pineapple in an airtight container (or freeze) to use in boozy smoothies or extra pineappley Piña Coladas (page 163) or as garnishes.*

Coconut Rum MAKES 1 (750-ML) BOTTLE
KNIFE OR BOX GRATER, SEALABLE LARGE GLASS JAR, CHEESECLOTH OR COFFEE FILTER, FUNNEL

1 whole, ripe coconut, chopped, or 3 cups freshly grated coconut
1 (750-ml) bottle white or dark rum

In a sealable large glass jar, combine the chopped white coconut meat and the rum. Seal and shake. Let stand at room temperature for 2 to 3 weeks, shaking often. Taste often to test the flavor intensity. Once it is to your taste, strain through cheesecloth or a coffee filter, funnel back into the original bottle, and label.

For all the flavor without the syrupy sweetness: *Few flavored liquors are quite as notorious as coconut rum. When made at home, the result tastes like fresh coconut meat and rum rather than a chemical-laden, overly sweet liqueur.*

Cherry Bounce MAKES 1 (750-ML) BOTTLE
LARGE SAUCEPAN, 2 SEALABLE LARGE GLASS JARS, FINE STRAINER, FUNNEL

6 cups whole cherries, preferably sour cherries
2 cups cane sugar
1 quart rum or rye whiskey

In a large saucepan over medium heat, bring the cherries and sugar to a simmer. Reduce the heat to medium-low and continue to simmer for 20 minutes, stirring occasionally. Remove from the heat and let cool. Pour the cooled cherry mixture into a sealable large glass jar, and add the rum or whiskey. Secure the lid, shake to combine, and let rest in a cool, dark place for 3 months. After 3 months, strain through a fine strainer, funnel into a clean glass jar, and label. If desired, reserve infused cherries for garnishing. The bounce will keep for up to 2 months.

A colonial-era treat: *This approach can be used to preserve many fruits and vegetables, but Cherry Bounce is the most historically significant: It was one of George Washington's favorite drinks.*

TEQUILA INFUSION RECIPES

Over recent years, tequila has become an incredibly nuanced category. Despite the depth, infusing tequila is still a lot of fun. Jalapeño tequila is probably the most popular, but a cool tequila cocktail is also delicious with berries, other fruits, and herbs. If you like the look of these recipes but avoid tequila, try substituting vodka or white rum.

Jalapeño Tequila MAKES 1 (750-ML) BOTTLE
KNIFE, SEALABLE LARGE GLASS JAR, CHEESECLOTH OR COFFEE FILTER, FUNNEL

1½ to 3 fresh jalapeños
1 (750-ml) bottle midgrade tequila

Thinly slice the jalapeños. For a milder heat, discard the seeds. Put both the slices, and seeds if using, in a sealable large glass jar. Pour in the tequila. Seal and shake. Let sit a few hours, and taste. For more spice, let sit overnight. When it is adequately spicy, strain out the solids using cheesecloth or a coffee filter, funnel into its original bottle, and label.

Strawberry Tequila MAKES 1 (750-ML) BOTTLE
KNIFE, SEALABLE LARGE GLASS JAR, CHEESECLOTH OR COFFEE FILTER, FUNNEL

1 pound strawberries, washed, hulled, and sliced
1 (750-ml) bottle midgrade tequila

Put the strawberry slices in a sealable large glass jar, and pour in the tequila. Seal and shake gently. Let sit at room temperature for 2 to 7 days, tasting often. If it steeps for more than 2 weeks, the strawberry taste may become perfumy. Strain through cheesecloth or a coffee filter, funnel into the original bottle, and label.

THE BAR

Ginger Tequila MAKES 1 (750-ML) BOTTLE
SEALABLE LARGE GLASS JAR, CHEESECLOTH OR COFFEE FILTER, FUNNEL

¾ cup thinly sliced ginger
1 (750-ml) bottle midgrade tequila

Put the ginger in a sealable large glass jar, and pour in the tequila. Seal and shake gently. Let sit at room temperature for 24 to 72 hours, shaking occasionally and tasting often after the first 24 hours. Strain through a cheesecloth or coffee filter, funnel into the original bottle, and label.

Watermelon Tequila MAKES 1 (750-ML) BOTTLE
SEALABLE LARGE GLASS JAR, CHEESECLOTH OR COFFEE FILTER, FUNNEL

1 small, seedless watermelon (about 2 pounds of 1-inch cubes)
1 (750-ml) bottle midgrade tequila

Put the watermelon in a sealable large glass jar. Pour in the tequila, seal the jar, and shake gently. Let sit at room temperature for at least 48 hours, and then taste frequently until it has the perfect amount of watermelon flavor. Strain through a cheesecloth or coffee filter, funnel into the original bottle, and label. If you so wish, set watermelon cubes aside in an airtight container to use in frozen margaritas.

VODKA INFUSION RECIPES

As a neutral spirit, vodka is the blank slate of the cocktail world. Adventurous souls have infused it with everything from bubblegum and Skittles to basil, strawberry, and everything in between. Likewise, vodka producers have put out hundreds of flavors. Not all use artificial flavoring, but many of them taste like sticky-sweet chemicals. As with the other recipes, these flavors are suggestions. Switch up your favorite citrusy drinks with herb or fruit flavors, or use the more savory flavors in Bloody Marys (page 192) or Vodka Martinis (page 118). Vodka is a vehicle for delivering other tastes, so use it early, often, and well.

Black Tea Vodka MAKES 1 (750-ML) BOTTLE
SEALABLE LARGE GLASS JAR, CHEESECLOTH OR COFFEE FILTER, FUNNEL

1 tablespoon black tea leaves
1 (750-ml) bottle vodka

Put the tea leaves in a sealable large glass jar, and pour in the vodka. Seal and shake to combine. Let steep for 2 to 3 hours. Strain through a cheesecloth or coffee filter to remove the tea, funnel into the original bottle, and label.

Cranberry Vodka MAKES 1 (750-ML) BOTTLE
SEALABLE LARGE GLASS JAR, CHEESECLOTH OR COFFEE FILTER, FUNNEL

1 pound fresh cranberries, washed
1 (750-ml) bottle vodka

Put the cranberries in a sealable 1½-liter glass jar. Seal, and shake to combine. Let sit for at least 1 week but up to 3, shaking frequently and tasting often. Once it has reached an acceptable level of cranberry flavoring, strain through a cheesecloth or coffee filter, funnel into the original bottle, and label. Enjoy in cocktails like the Cosmopolitan (page 193).

Peppercorn Vodka MAKES 1 (750-ML) BOTTLE
SEALABLE LARGE GLASS JAR, CHEESECLOTH OR COFFEE FILTER, FUNNEL

2 tablespoons peppercorns, slightly cracked
1 (750-ml) bottle vodka

Put the peppercorns in a sealable 1½-liter glass jar, and pour in the vodka. Seal and shake to combine. Let sit for at least a week. Strain through a cheesecloth or coffee filter, funnel into the original bottle, and label. Pepper vodka is especially delicious in a Bloody Mary (page 192).

Horseradish Vodka MAKES 1 (750-ML) BOTTLE
KNIFE, SEALABLE LARGE GLASS JAR, CHEESECLOTH OR COFFEE FILTER, FUNNEL

8 ounces fresh horseradish root, peeled and thinly sliced
2 teaspoons black peppercorns
1 (750-ml) bottle vodka

Put the horseradish slices and peppercorns in a sealable large glass jar, and pour in the vodka. Seal and shake to combine. Let sit for at least 24 hours. Taste at the end of the first day. If spicy enough, strain though a cheesecloth or coffee filter, funnel into the original bottle, and label.

BITTERS

If you compare a bartender's set of tools against a chef's, the bartender's bitters selection is the closest thing to the chef's spice rack. Like culinary spices, bitters add complex flavors and balance to a drink as a whole. A dash or two of bitters can also balance a cocktail by curbing its sweetness. But if bitter tastes are not your favorite, no worries—despite the name, a dash or two will not turn your whole drink bitter.

Though the variety of bitters available is almost astounding, they are pretty simple. Bitters are basically highly concentrated infusions of herbs and spices. In the days before pharmaceutical medicine, bitters were sold as cure-alls or stomach medicines. Hundreds of brands of bitters were available, and traveling salesmen hawked their wares all over the United States.

Unfortunately, there was no science to back up their claims. Once the United States government began regulating products claiming to have medicinal value, most bitters brands were run out of business. What the legislation did not kill, Prohibition did, leaving only Angostura behind. Now, thanks to renewed interest in cocktails, other brands have gotten their start, and more continue to pop up every month. Flavors now range from spicy pepper to citrus and Angostura-like aromatics.

It is not uncommon for bars and home bartenders to make their own bitters. Aside from their utility in creating house cocktails, bitters also make great gifts. As with other types of infusions, vodka may seem like the go-to base. But, as long as you use a high-proof spirit, other liquors may be better suited for different types of bitters. You can experiment with how the base liquor affects the end product. One note: Many of the herbs or dried plants in these recipes do not come in small quantities, so batching in small quantities may be difficult. Consider hosting a bitters-making party and sharing the wealth.

BITTERS RECIPES

Orange Bitters   MAKES ABOUT 6 CUPS

Other than aromatic bitters, orange bitters are arguably the most versatile. Once strained, they will last almost forever.
3 SEALABLE LARGE GLASS JARS, CHEESECLOTH OR COFFEE FILTER, SMALL SAUCEPAN, FUNNEL, SMALL BOTTLES WITH DROPPERS

2 cups grain alcohol
1 cup dried orange peel, chopped finely with all pith (white stuff) removed
1 teaspoon cardamom seeds
1 teaspoon coriander seeds
1 teaspoon quassia chips
½ teaspoon caraway seeds
½ teaspoon powdered cinchona bark
¼ teaspoon gentian root
½ cup water
2 tablespoons Rich Simple Syrup (page 44)

Put the alcohol, orange peel, cardaom, coriander, quassia chips, caraway, cinchona bark, gentian root, and the water in a sealable large glass jar with ½ cup water. Push the dry ingredients down so that they are covered by liquid. Seal the jar. Shake vigorously once a day for 2 weeks. Strain the mixture through a cheesecloth or coffee filter into a large, clean, sealable glass jar. Set this jar aside. Put the strained-out solids in a small saucepan, and cover with water. Bring to a boil over medium-high heat, and then lower the heat and simmer for 10 minutes. Remove the pan from the heat, and allow to cool completely. Add the contents to a clean glass jar, cover, and store for 1 week, shaking daily. Strain through a cheesecloth into a clean glass jar. Discard the solids, and combine this liquid with the alcoholic mixture in the jar you set aside. Add the Rich Simple Syrup. Shake to combine, and then let sit at room temperature for 3 days. Skim any debris off of its surface, strain one last time, funnel into small bottles with droppers, and label.

Aromatic Bitters MAKES ABOUT 3 CUPS

Just the basics, ma'am. These can be used in recipes that call for Angostura.

VEGETABLE PEELER, 2 SEALABLE LARGE GLASS JARS, FUNNEL, SMALL BOTTLES WITH DROPPERS

1 medium lemon
1 (750-ml) bottle overproof grain alcohol
40 drops gentian extract
1 teaspoon whole black peppercorns
1 (3-inch) cinnamon stick
1 (1½-inch) piece fresh ginger, halved
4 whole allspice berries
4 whole cloves

Using a vegetable peeler, remove the lemon zest in strips, leaving the white pith behind. (Use the fruit in another application.) In a sealable large glass jar, combine the lemon zest and all the remaining ingredients. Seal and store at room temperature. Let steep for 2 weeks, shaking the jar every other day. Strain the mixture through a cheesecloth or coffee filter into another large glass jar, funnel into small bottles with droppers, and label.

Chocolate Bitters MAKES ABOUT 4 CUPS

3 SEALABLE 16-OUNCE GLASS JARS, CHEESECLOTH OR A COFFEE FILTER,
FUNNEL, SMALL BOTTLES WITH DROPPERS

½ cup cacao nibs
2½ cups 100 proof bourbon, divided
2 tonka beans, cracked
6 cardamom pods, chopped
1 cinnamon stick
½ vanilla bean, split
1 tablespoon gentian root
1 tablespoon sarsaparilla
1 teaspoon wild cherry bark
1 teaspoon cassia chips
1 teaspoon black walnut leaf
1 cup 100 proof rye whiskey
¼ cup Simple Syrup (page 44)

Add the cocoa nibs and 1¼ cups of bourbon to a sealable 16-ounce
glass jar, and shake well. In a second sealable 16-ounce glass jar,
combine the tonka beans, cardamom pods, cinnamon stick, split
vanilla bean, and the remaining 1¼ cup of bourbon. In a third sealable
16-ounce glass jar, combine the gentian root, sarsaparilla, wild cherry
bark, cassia chips, black walnut leaf, and whiskey. Store all 3 jars out
of direct sunlight, shaking each once per day for 5 days.

Strain the jar with the whiskey mix through cheesecloth or a coffee
filter. Clean the jar, and pour the strained liquid back in. Discard the
solids. After 10 days, strain the other two jars, discarding the solids,
and combine the liquid of those 2 jars into 1. Let sit for 3 days. Strain
both jars again, adding the Simple Syrup to your bourbon mixture.
Combine small portions of both mixtures until the bitterness levels are
to your liking. Funnel into small bottles with droppers, label, and let
sit for 1 week.

SYRUPS

Syrups have become a ubiquitous part of cocktail culture. But in the centuries before refrigeration, syrups were impractical unless they could be used within a few days. As a result, recipes from this era usually call for sugar rather than syrup. However, using sugar has a few pitfalls. First, if the sugar is not dissolved before ice is added, it is probably going to leave a sticky layer. Second, it is less consistent: You cannot precisely control how much of the sugar will dissolve, whereas you can control the sugar content with syrup. For these reasons, almost all the recipes in this book are written using syrup rather than sugar.

Syrups, like garnishes, are another infinitely customizable way to spruce up your cocktails. You can make syrup from agave, honey, or brown sugar and steep spices or fruits in the syrup to add different flavors. You can even play around with the amount of sugar you add to make the syrup more or less sweet. The possibilities are endless. In a pinch, you can muddle about 1 sugar cube or teaspoon of sugar per ½ ounce of simple syrup into the drink, to taste, but we suggest going straight for the good stuff.

Though several syrup-making companies have popped up, quality products are going to cost you. If you do plan to buy your syrups, avoid products containing artificial color or flavoring. They will not taste the same. But in the time it takes to go to the supermarket, you could just make it yourself for a fraction of the cost.

SIMPLE SYRUP RECIPE

From its straightforward recipe to its easy ingredients, simple syrup is one of the most basic bar staples. By definition, it is a mixture of one part granulated cane sugar and one part water. And it is easy to make: Combine 1 cup sugar and 1 cup hot water in a clean container. Stir until the sugar is entirely dissolved. (You can also combine sugar with room-temperature water, but the process takes a bit longer and is not as shelf stable.) *Each of these syrup recipes makes about 1½ cups.*

Vanilla Simple Syrup: Mix 1 cup sugar with 1 cup boiling water and about 15 drops vanilla extract. Stir until sugar has entirely dissolved.

Rich Simple Syrup: To make rich simple syrup that will last longer, use 2 cups sugar for every cup of hot water.

Demerara Syrup: Substitute demerara sugar for sugar in the Rich Simple Syrup recipe.

Rich Demerara Syrup: Use 2 cups demerara sugar for every cup of hot water.

Honey Syrup: Combine 1 cup honey and 1 cup hot water. Stir until the honey is entirely dissolved and then let cool. Seal tightly and refrigerate for up to 2 months.

Maple Syrup: Typically found in more modern cocktails, maple syrup should be used without any water added. Grade B is preferable and is most often used in cooking. The grade comes from its color rather than quality.

FLAVORED SYRUP RECIPES

Syrups can be flavored by infusion or the use of liquid ingredients like tea or juices. But the variety that those options create is endless. Start with some of the recipes below to get the techniques down, and experiment with how the fresh versions impact the flavor of classic cocktails.

Grenadine   MAKES ABOUT 1½ CUPS

Use instead of the artificially colored stuff in a New York Cocktail (page 235) or Hurricane (page 152).
SEALABLE GLASS JAR

1 cup pomegranate juice
1 cup sugar

In a sealable glass jar, combine the pomegranate juice (Pom works best) and sugar. Shake, allow to settle, and shake again. Repeat until all sugar is dissolved. Label the jar, and refrigerate for up to 1 month.

Ginger Syrup   MAKES ABOUT 1½ CUPS

For a bit of spice, use Ginger Syrup in a Pimm's Cup (page 134), Gimlet (page 117), or Whiskey Sour (page 221).
SMALL SAUCEPAN, FUNNEL, FINE STRAINER, SEALABLE GLASS JAR OR BOTTLE

1 cup ginger juice
1 cup sugar

In a small saucepan over high heat, bring the ginger juice to a boil. Add the sugar, stir, and turn off the heat. Allow the mixture to cool. Funnel the mixture though a fine strainer into a sealable glass jar or bottle, and label.

Orgeat MAKES ABOUT 1½ CUPS

Though it may seem simply like an almond-flavored syrup, orgeat brings more to Mai Tais (page 161) than a flavor extract added to simple syrup. Though it is available from some producers, it takes about 15 minutes of labor to make your own.

BAKING SHEET, BLENDER OR FOOD PROCESSOR, MEDIUM SAUCEPAN, CHEESECLOTH, LARGE BOWL, FUNNEL

2 cups raw almonds, sliced or chopped
1½ cups sugar
1¼ cups water
1 teaspoon orange flower water
1 ounce vodka

Preheat the oven to 400 degrees Fahrenheit. Spread the almonds on a baking sheet and toast for 4 minutes, shaking after 2 minutes. Cool the almonds, and then pulverize them with a blender or food processor. In a medium saucepan over medium heat, heat the sugar and water until the sugar dissolves and the mixture starts to boil, about 3 minutes, stirring constantly. Add the pulverized almonds, turn the heat down to low, and simmer, stirring frequently. When the mixture is about to boil, remove from the heat and cover. Let sit for a minimum of 3 hours and no more than 12 hours. Strain the steeped mixture through three layers of cheesecloth into a bowl, squeezing the cloth as you go. Add the orange flower water and vodka to the bowl, and stir. Funnel into a glass jar or bottle, and label.

Pineapple Syrup   MAKES ABOUT 2½ CUPS

Substitute for simple syrup in a Daiquiri (page 151), Pisco Sour (page 79), or gin drink for a fruity and refreshing twist.
VEGETABLE PEELER, KNIFE, FINE STRAINER, SEALABLE LARGE GLASS JAR

4 cups sugar
2 cups water
1 small pineapple, peeled and cubed

In a large bowl, stir to combine the sugar and water. Add the pineapple cubes to the syrup. Let sit for 24 hours. Remove the fruit, but lightly juice the cubes into the bowl to add some juice to the mixture. Stir again to dissolve any remaining sugar, and pour through a fine strainer into a sealable large glass jar. Label, and keep refrigerated for up to 1 month.

Hibiscus Syrup   MAKES ABOUT 1½ CUPS

Though you can use dried hibiscus flowers, herbal teas made with these ingredients may be easier to find. Use in place of simple syrup in rum drinks like the Daiquiri (page 151), or spice up vodka cocktails.
SMALL SAUCEPAN, SEALABLE GLASS JAR

1 cup water
5 hibiscus tea bags
1 cup sugar

In a small saucepan over high heat, bring the water to a boil. Add the tea bags, cover, and let steep for 5 minutes. Remove the tea bags, squeeze, and discard. Mix in the sugar, stirring until dissolved. Store in a sealable glass jar, labeled, for up to 1 month.

Though the glassware shapes the drink, the garnish provides the visual appeal. A stunning presentation can make a cocktail almost irresistible—just think about mai tais festooned with orchid blossoms, banana dolphins riding tiki drinks, and the oh-so-cool olive in a martini. These drinks would not look or taste the same without the decoration. But within the bar world, garniture depends on the bar. Some subscribe to a no-garnish policy, opting to add the flavor without the visual impact. At home, it is completely up to you. Playing around with garnishes is also a great way to personalize a cocktail. If the lime wedge is not your style, replace it! Experiment with an orange wedge, carved lime peel, or cocktail umbrella until you find something you love.

Aside from the purely aesthetic aspect, garnishes also bring a final flavor to a drink. An orange peel adds a citrusy element to an old fashioned, while a lime wedge lets a guest tweak their daiquiri to perfection. A maraschino cherry adds a final bit of sweetness to a Manhattan, and an olive adds a touch of saltiness that cuts any bitterness in a martini.

Cherries: In the nineteenth century, maraschino cherries were not fluorescent red. Instead, they were tart Croatian cherries preserved in liqueur. As the cost of production rose, companies began substituting locally available ingredients. By Prohibition, chemicals had replaced the liqueur, leading to the violently red fruits of today. Look for naturally preserved cherries like Luxardo brand.

Flamed orange peel: Though this technique can be used with lemon peels, orange peels work better. Cut a wide swath of peel from the orange. Do not worry about getting too much pith. Strike a long-stemmed match, and hold it in your nondominant hand. Holding the peel in your dominant hand, heat the peel by bringing the colorful side about 2 inches away from the flame. If some soot gets on the peel, you have brought it too close, but it can still be used. Holding the match tip between the peel and the drink, about 5 inches away from the drink's surface, squeeze the peel so it bends toward the flame. Rub the peel around the rim and drop it in or discard, per the cocktail recipe's directive.

Nutmeg and other spices: Some wintery drinks will have you sprinkle nutmeg or other spices on the surface to finish them off. Many of these are also commonly used in baking, so check your pantry before you run to the store.

Olives and onions: Olives and onions add a touch of saltiness to a drink. Fortunate or not, there is no real substitute for their presence.

Salt rim: Cut a wedge of lime. Rub the wedge around the edge of the glass. Pour enough salt to generously coat a plate, and run the edge of the glass through the salt.

Sugar rim: Cut a wedge of lemon. Rub the wedge around the edge of the glass. Pour enough sugar to generously coat a plate, and run the edge of the glass through the sugar.

Spirals: Using a channel knife or paring knife, start at one end of a citrus fruit to cut a continuous, narrow strip of peel. It should come off as a spiral, but to shape, wrap it around your finger and drop it slowly into the drink.

Twists: Using a vegetable peeler or paring knife, start at one end of a citrus fruit and cut a wide strip of peel lengthwise. Twist the peel above the surface of the drink with the colorful side toward the beverage to release its oils. Rub the rind around the edge of the drink, and drop it in or discard.

Wheels: Cut rounds of fruits or vegetables crosswise. Do not limit yourself to citrus—starfruit and other not-round tropical fruits look really cool when cut like this.

Sugared fruit slices: Sugared fruit slices are commonly used in shots. Cut a lemon, lime, or orange into wedges. Pour sugar into a bowl, and coat both sides of the fruit in sugar.

CHAPTER TWO

THE ART

Anatomy of a Cocktail

What exactly is a cocktail? If you take stock in one of the first published definitions of a cocktail, then you would say that it must be a "stimulating liquor, composed of spirits of any kind, sugar, water, and bitters" (*The Balance and Columbian Repository*, V no. 19 May 13, 1806: page 146).

But if you take that definition at face value, a screwdriver is not a cocktail, because it lacks sugar and bitters. Neither is a gimlet or hot toddy, and certainly not a piña colada, for all these lack bitters. So, let us look for a broader definition. The most fitting is to break the cocktail into three parts: its base, body, and modifier.

The base: Typically, the base is the main alcoholic ingredient used in the largest quantity. For example, the base for a Manhattan is rye whiskey, which makes it a whiskey drink. There is one huge exception to this rule: equal-parts cocktails like the Negroni (page 119), the Blood and Sand (page 224), or even the Long Island Iced Tea (page 201) where two (or more) bases are used in equal measure. (Every rule is meant to be broken.)

The body: The ingredients that make up the body change the flavor but do not overwhelm the base spirit. Usually, they follow a ratio or set pattern and constitute the bulk of what you are drinking. They also normally supply the texture and much of the drink's consistency.

The modifier: Technically speaking, anything added to a spirit is a modifier. Often, they add flavors that enrich the drink as a whole by adding subtle, complementary flavors rather than making up the main architecture of the drink. Playing with modifiers is also the easiest way to start experimenting with cocktails. Use an aromatic bitter that is not Angostura in an Old Fashioned (page 219), or add a dash of orange bitters to a Bee's Knees (page 122). Potential variations are endless. Some call modifiers the perfume.

- **Example:** the Manhattan
- **Base:** rye whiskey
- **Body:** sweet vermouth
- **Modifier:** bitters

Preparing Your Bar

When you entertain, no one will expect you to flip shakers or pour flaming drinks. But your guests will want something to sip. Despite the huge number of existing articles detailing how to stock your bar, there is no one-size-fits-all answer. Your needs will vary from your next-door neighbor's, but having a basic setup on hand at all times will ensure that you are ready for anything. For many, a minimalist setup will provide everything needed to make most cocktails and shooters that they will enjoy. Some overachievers will want to completely stock their bars from the get-go.

The most important rule to remember is to keep what you like—and will drink—on hand. As much as you may enjoy experimenting, there is nothing like being able to fall back on old favorites. There is a second part to this rule. Though conventional wisdom holds that liquor never spoils, it does change as it ages. If you or your guests are not going to drink it, it is never going to move from your shelf.

You will eventually want to get at least one 750-milliliter bottle of every major type of liquor. If you are just starting out, the first bottle you get should be something you like, whether that is vodka, Scotch, or rum. Next, branch into a category that you like but are less familiar with. If you are starting with vodka, pick up a vodka-like rum like Don Q. If Scotch is more your speed, track down a quality mezcal like Del Maguey Single Village. Check out some recipes or sip them in place of your go-to. From there, begin moving toward cocktails that seem unfamiliar, or are one step away from something you absolutely love.

When you are starting to really experiment with things you do not readily have on hand, buy a smaller 375-milliliter bottle or something similar. I have included some brand recommendations with the introductions to each liquor chapter. These are based on my personal experience and taste and may not be your favorites. If and when you want to branch out further, ask a bartender you trust what they would choose. Also note that more expensive options may seem swankier (or prettier), but there are often others that are just as good or better for less money.

Further, few bartenders keep a fully stocked bar at home. Keeping equipment and liquor on hand will help, but it may often be easier to buy citrus and make syrup as needed. Most importantly no matter what anyone or any book may tell you, there is no single definition of what constitutes a "stocked" bar.

Measurements and Portioning

Mixing cocktails is like baking: Precisely measuring ingredients has a noticeable effect on the end product. Though many bartenders practice free pouring, or the art of mixing cocktails without jiggers, it can lead to a lot of inconsistencies without a lot of practice. Recipes in this book are measured in fluid ounces, but older books will use measurements like fingers, wineglasses, ponies, or jiggers. Others use ratios, which you may still notice in a fair number of cocktails included here.

HOW TO MEASURE

In terms of pouring ingredients for mixing, most bartenders follow the same steps. If the recipe calls for bitters, add those first. Then add syrup. Make sure that you always measure so that the jigger or measuring spoon is almost overflowing. Since a bit of residue will be left in the measuring device, this will ensure that you end up with the same amount every time. Next, add the juice (and fill the jigger to the brim). Next, add liqueurs or wine-based products, and then the base (or most expensive) liquor. That way, if you mess up, you are throwing out the least expensive parts.

PORTIONING

Outside of the punches, all the recipes in this book are written to make one drink. With a little bit of math and some ice, all of them can be

THE CLASSIC & CRAFT COCKTAIL RECIPE BOOK

scaled up to make a pitcher or more. At parties, this will get you out from behind the bar and make sure your guests enjoy their drinks. Just choose a drink that will not separate and does not have a lot of herbs or other ingredients that could turn brown. Drinks made with eggs, blended drinks, and muddled drinks can be batched, but none of those types of drinks stay appetizing once mixed. Once you have chosen your cocktail, multiply each measurement by the number of drinks you wish to make, convert ounces to cups, and mix in a pitcher. Add ice, stir vigorously, and serve over ice, regardless of whether the original drink called for ice.

Techniques for Superior Drinks

In cocktail-making, attention to detail is everything. As long as the ingredients are carefully measured and promptly strained, the result should be a balanced, well-executed cocktail. Aside from that, cocktail technique is a matter of making the cocktail's production a beautiful and ergonomic process. The ergonomic side is more important for professional bartenders, but for home bartenders, it is a matter of beautiful presentation more than anything else. If you have questions about the techniques bartenders use to create new cocktails, flip to "Craft Your Own" (page 62).

MUDDLING

Many cocktails call for muddled fruit or herbs. When using mint and other delicate herbs, gently press the leaves against the walls or bottom of your vessel just until you can smell them. Smashing herbs too far into a pulp breaks the leaves' veins, resulting in bitter, earthy flavors. But for fruits, smash away. Crushing them releases the juices inside and oils on their surfaces.

THE ART

CHILLING GLASSWARE

There's nothing worse than a drink that is warmed to room temperature before it is empty. One of the easiest techniques for preventing that from happening quickly is chilling the glass. That way, the newly shaken or stirred beverage is not immediately warmed by the glassware. Though a drinker's hand will warm the glass over time, that effect is mitigated by a cold glass. Chilling the vessel also provides a visual confirmation that the drink inside is at the correct temperature before you take a sip.

SHAKING VS. STIRRING

Making a Bond joke about shaking and stirring is easy, but explaining why some drinks are shaken and others stirred is more complicated. Generally, cocktails made with citrus, egg whites, or any form of dairy are shaken, whereas spirituous (booze only) tipples are stirred. Though the defining characteristics may seem arbitrary, the two techniques result in completely different cocktails. If you ever get the chance, taste a shaken margarita and a stirred one side by side. The difference is astounding.

Why the difference? Shaking adds about three times more water to a drink than stirring. Even with a short shake, these cocktails are more diluted and much colder. For drinks with citrus, cream, or other strongly flavored ingredients, the added agitation blends the tastes well. Perhaps most important, shaking changes the appearance of your cocktail. For drinks with citrus or dairy in them, shaking folds in air that creates a fresh, frothy texture. But for jewel-toned or brown spirituous drinks, adding that much air may make these drinks look like churned-up puddles. The appearance of a drink affects how it tastes on a psychological level, and a visually unappetizing cocktail is more likely to be perceived as tasting unpleasant as well. Ultimately, it is up to you. Use your best judgment, and prioritize the approaches that make cocktails taste best to you.

To shake well, shake confidently, holding one end of the shaker tin in each hand firmly. To stir, use the bar spoon to move the ice. Many

THE CLASSIC & CRAFT COCKTAIL RECIPE BOOK

bartenders will advocate the Japanese technique of keeping the back of the bowl of the spoon against the wall of the mixing glass and gently moving the ice, but when you are at home, there is no wrong way to stir.

BLENDING

Aside from mixing chilly cocktails, a blender can be used to purée fruits, quickly crush ice into a smoothie or piña colada, or make large batches of these chilly concoctions. If you are ever making frozen versions of other cocktails, be sure to increase the amount of flavorful ingredients like spirits, citrus, and syrups, because melting ice will water them down. Crushed ice is best for blending, as it can be broken down more evenly than whole cubes. For the best drinks, add ice first, and then pour other ingredients on top. Blend on low speed for a few seconds, and then increase to high speed for a smooth finish.

FLOATING

Armed with a spoon and a bit of patience, floating is a technique within almost any home bartender's reach. It is typically used with drinks containing cream or liqueurs. To float such an ingredient, pour it slowly over the back of the spoon near the surface of the drink. Once poured, the liquid should float on top.

DECORATING

The craft cocktail boom has pioneered countless innovations in the different ways that cocktails can be decorated. Fancy swizzle sticks and exotic fruits are not uncommon features, but neither are patterns stenciled with bitters in egg white foam. At home, you can still make stunning cocktails: Pour bitters into a 2- to 4-ounce misting spray bottle. Mist a spritz or two over the top of a drink for an ombré effect, or use an eyedropper to place drops of bitters on egg foam; then, using a toothpick, trace designs through the bitters.

CHAPTER THREE

THE CRAFT

What Is a Craft Cocktail?

Before Prohibition, there was no need for the term *craft cocktails*. Tending bar was a respectable occupation that required a lot of training. Some recipes and techniques were written down, but many more were passed from bartender to bartender through the oral tradition. With the start of the Noble Experiment, most of these skilled bartenders left the field or the country for more welcoming jobs.

Though the (legal) bar business sprang back quickly after Prohibition was repealed, irreparable damage had been done. Since most pre-Prohibition bartenders had left the craft, many techniques such as shaking and stirring, and even more, history, such as how citrus peel garnishes got their start, were lost. Further, public taste had shifted toward sweeter drinks, and many of the complex imported ingredients used in older cocktails were not brought back into the country. Sour mix, which at that time was a mixture of citrus juice, sugar, and water with something to make it shelf stable, was being marketed as an edgy new product.

The result was a gradual shift away from balanced, nuanced cocktails. By the 1960s, super-sweet drinks made with sour mix and vodka were beginning to take hold. Some drinks, like the daiquiri, were sweetened and rejiggered into neon-hued blended concoctions. Others were forgotten entirely. This trend continued until the mid-1990s, when some bartenders and aficionados began experimenting with old recipes and fresh ingredients. As a result, some bartenders refer to these decades as the Dark Ages of Cocktails.

Nowadays, the resuscitated tipples are often referred to as *craft cocktails*. Most of the time, these are made with ingredients and processes that approximate how bartenders in the 1800s would have mixed out of necessity: fresh juices, homemade syrups and bitters, seasonal produce, and elegant technique. Though you do not have to perfect these techniques to make delicious drinks, confident preparation and quality ingredients will go a long way in convincing others you have got it all figured out.

Ice: Many bartenders will tell you that ice is their equivalent to a chef's stove. Using differently shaped ice cubes for each drink when appropriate will render an aesthetically pleasing effect while also contributing to making each drink exactly how you want it.

Seasonal inspiration: Within the culinary world, menus based on seasonal ingredients are old hat. Though it is slightly newer to bartending, the huge variety of ingredients available can be the perfect inspiration. For example, cranberry juice, allspice liqueur, smoky Scotch, aged rum, and many other darker flavors will warm you through in winter. Summer's heat calls more for light, citrusy, or soda-topped libations. Mix and match for spring and fall.

Homemade syrup: Syrups are the easiest and cheapest cocktail ingredient to make at home, either for personal use or gifting. For most parties, you can get away with stocking basic simple syrup. (For a recipe, see page 44.) Many other syrups like grenadine, demer-ara, or pineapple syrup are pretty simple, even though they sound impressive. (See pages 45, 44, or 47, respectively.) Since these will keep for a month or more in the fridge, they add texture and rich sweetness to last-minute cocktails with friends or batching punches for lavish parties.

Juices: Buying presqueezed juices at the store is convenient. Unfor-tunately, most commercial citrus juices have preservatives that make them as bitter as if they had been left in the fridge for a week. For crisp, fresh flavor in your citrus cocktails, keep the whole citrus fruit on hand both for garnishes and juice. While bowls of citrus make great decorations, they also allow you to make every drink fresh. For best results, squeeze your juice within 24 hours of making drinks.

Infusions: Bitters and other infusions are a fantastic way to per-sonalize many drinks. If you make vanilla vodka, you can dress up a screwdriver or Moscow mule with some new flavors. Spicy tequila takes a margarita to a new level. But bitters are a big part of this world as well. Making your own house bitters (page 39) and using a bit of syrup can make a killer old fashioned or a new spin on the whiskey sour. The flavor combinations are endless.

THE CRAFT

Garnishes: Every bartender has an opinion about garnishes. Whether a drink is served with just the oils from the peel on its surface or the peel itself is dropped in, garnishes add both a visual element to drinks as well as a tiny tweak to their flavors. Classic garnishes are often minimal, while tiki garnishes such as banana dolphin and pineapple can jump the shark. As with most other elements, it is completely up to you how, or even if, you garnish your drinks.

Craft Your Own

Though classic and modern craft cocktails may taste as if they were divinely inspired, the large majority are loosely based on one of four formats. By working through the recipes in this book, you will find out a lot about what you like and what you do not. Making drinks will give you some clues on how to begin crafting your own.

Though it may sound counterintuitive, do not start from scratch. Instead, start from a basic recipe you know and like. When you are starting out, use the templates on the following pages to begin experimenting with new combinations of flavors you like. Use them to modify existing cocktails or to create your own. They should be used as starting points: Adding bitters or playing with the exact measurements is part of the learning process. Below are some suggestions for each type of ingredient.

- **Possible sweet ingredients:** syrup, liqueur, freshly squeezed orange juice
- **Sour:** lemon, lime, grapefruit juice
- **Bubbles:** soda, ginger beer, champagne, sparkling wine

THE CLASSIC & CRAFT COCKTAIL RECIPE BOOK

The Sour

COUPE GLASS | JIGGER, SHAKER, HAWTHORNE STRAINER

1 ounce sweet
1 ounce sour
2 ounces liquor

Shake all ingredients with ice until chilled through. Strain into a chilled coupe glass and serve.

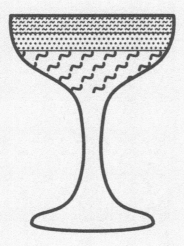

Improved Cocktail

ROCKS GLASS | KNIFE, JIGGER, MIXING GLASS, BAR SPOON,
HAWTHORNE STRAINER

1 to 3 dashes bitters
¼ ounce syrup
¼ ounce liqueur (optional)
2 ounces liquor
Citrus peel, for garnish

In a mixing glass, stir the liquid ingredients with ice until
chilled. Strain into a chilled rocks glass, garnish with the
citrus peel, and serve.

THE CLASSIC & CRAFT COCKTAIL RECIPE BOOK

The Collins

COLLINS GLASS | JIGGER, SHAKER, HAWTHORNE STRAINER

1 ounce sweet
1 ounce sour
2 ounces liquor
Something bubbly, for topping

Shake the first three ingredients with ice until chilled through.
Strain into a chilled Collins glass filled with ice, top with
something bubbly, and serve.

Manhattan

COCKTAIL GLASS | KNIFE, JIGGER, MIXING GLASS, BAR SPOON,
HAWTHORNE STRAINER

2 ounces whiskey
1 ounce fortified wine
1 to 3 dashes bitters
Citrus peel, for garnish

In a mixing glass, stir the liquid ingredients with ice until
chilled. Strain into a chilled cocktail glass, garnish with the
citrus peel, and serve.

THE CLASSIC & CRAFT COCKTAIL RECIPE BOOK

Other Modifications

In each cocktail, you can use more than one ingredient for each sweet, sour, or liquor. If you are using two sweeteners in a Collins, split the sweetener by using ½ ounce of each. Likewise, if you want to use two liquors, use 1 ounce of each.

Make sure to change just one thing every time you make the drink and to write down the changes you make. That way, if you make a fantastic cocktail or the recipe starts to go wrong, you will know what you did differently.

Troubleshooting

Making subpar drinks is part of the learning process. Since every person's ideal cocktail is different, what is perfect for you could be too bitter or too tart for someone else. Instead of dumping an imperfect drink, next time, try to tweak your creation. Here is how:

- **Too sweet?** Add a dash of bitters. Citrus or orange bitters will pair well with drinks with juice in them.
- **Too bitter?** Add the tiniest pinch of salt. Many cocktail bars stock a saline solution that can be added in drops to curb bitterness. Even at levels where the saltiness is imperceptible, it is still working on your taste buds.
- **Too much bite or too sour?** Add a bit of sugar. It is a trick that vodka makers use to lessen the alcohol burn, and it works in cocktails.

PART TWO

The Recipes

CHAPTER FOUR

BRANDY

Its name conjures mental images of men in cravats swirling amber liquor in snifters while sitting in armchairs by a bearskin rug and roaring fire. Despite its luxe reputation, brandy is often considered a warming, fortifying dram. Though it is made pretty much anywhere fruit is grown, the best-known brandies are from France. Like the wine produced in France, the Cognacs and Armagnacs are the height of spirituous attainment.

LIKE WINE, BRANDY CAN BE MADE from any type of fruit, but grape-based brandies are the best known. When it was first distilled, it was called *brandewijn,* which translates literally to "burnt wine." Like early whiskies, this brandy was probably quite rough around the edges. It was also a novel product—the unaged spirit was nicknamed eau-de-vie and aquavit in different countries, which both translate to "water of life."

In the United States and around the world, brandy has been a constant in drinking culture. Until the 1860s, locally made brandies would have been the drink of choice for the upper middle class. That is, except in the Northeast, where rum was king (see page 144).

Early on, European producers figured out that barrel aging was a great way to smooth brandy's rough edges and shape the young spirit. Today, aging and blending brandy is a true art form, much as it is for whiskeys. But quality brandies hail from all over the world, with round South American piscos, gorgeous Californian fruit brandies, spicy Spanish brandies, and American applejack all making appearances in classic cocktails. Though there are many, many different types and legal classifications, here are the basics of brandy.

Types of Brandy

GRAPE-BASED BRANDIES

Armagnac: After being distilled once from white wine grapes, Armagnac is typically aged in barrels made from local French oak. It is typically aged longer than Cognac but tends to be slightly cheaper. Legally produced in Gascony, just to the south of Cognac, Armagnac is best enjoyed in a champagne glass or Glencairn. Most of the time, Armagnac is made in small batches by smaller producers, but it legally follows the same age indicators as Cognac and Calvados.

Cognac: Despite its deep heritage, Cognac is largely dominated by four houses: Courvoisier, Hennessy, Martell, and Rémy Martin. Many products from these producers are made to be commercially uniform and are produced with additives to make them pass quality-control standards. There are also some smaller producers making small batches.

Within the legally defined Cognac-producing region, there are six main zones: Grande Champagne, Petite Champagne, Borderies, Fins Bois, Bons Bois, and Bois Ordinaires. Chalky soil in the Grande Champagne region typically leads to the most elegant (sometimes called the best) Cognacs, while more clay content, as in the Borderies, gives a fuller product. But the most important part of production is the aging process. One note: Bottles labeled as *fine champagne* contain at least 50 percent product from the Grande Champagne region. Legally, it must spend at least two years in a barrel, though some spend more than two decades. But the location of the cellar, moisture exposure, and other elements can create stunningly different products.

Typically, Cognac is made by blending different vintages of brandy into one product. These are labeled with the region where they are made and either stars or an abbreviation designating the age of the youngest spirit inside. Three stars indicates it has been aged for at least 2 years, while VS, or "Very Special," represents the same. VSOP, or "very superior old pale," has been aged for at least 4 years. XO, or "extra old," also called Napoleon, has been matured for 6 years, while Hors d'Âge, "outside or beyond age," is subject to the same rules as XO but has usually been aged for longer. These strange English names most likely originated because the English were an integral part of the Cognac trade, especially in the eighteenth century.

Pisco brandy: Depending on whom you ask, pisco brandy hails from either Peru or Chile. Both countries have designated the liquor as their national spirit, and what is made in Peru cannot be labeled as pisco in Chile and vice versa. However, the climate in each region varies dramatically. While Chilean grapes are tended in a low-humidity environment and usually watered by drip irrigation, Peruvian grapes experience a climate closer to the ocean and are watered by flood irrigation.

Legal requirements for each are likewise different. In Chile, pisco may be distilled as many times as the producer wishes, while in Peru, pisco must be distilled and bottled straight off the still. Taste-wise, the variations range quite a bit, making attempts to describe exact attributes extremely difficult. Either way, it is delicious in a Pisco Sour (page 79).

Spanish brandy: Spanish brandy is often considered one of the most overlooked brandy categories on the market. Most brandy from Spain comes from Jerez, a region known for its sherry-making. There, brandy is made mostly from the same types of grapes used for sherry and labeled as Brandy de Jerez. As with sherry, some producers use the solera technique (see page 252). The aging classification varies slightly from its French equivalent: *Solera* is typically aged for about a year, *solera reserva* has an average age of 3 years, and *solera gran reserva* has an average age of 10 years.

Weinbrand: This German grape-based brandy must be aged for at least 6 months. If it is aged longer than a year, it can be labeled as *Alter Weinbrand* or VSOP. Much of the time, it is produced from wines purchased from other brandy-producing regions. Some are very similar to French brandies, especially those made with wine from Grande Champagne.

FRUIT BRANDY

As one might expect, a fruit brandy is made from any fruit—except grapes. With that said, outside the United States, fruit brandy may also be made from the seeds and stems of grapes, which are left over as a by-product of the winemaking process. Strangely enough, in Britain, the term may also include some cordials. There, it is more common to refer to the fruit-based spirits as eau-de-vie.

Applejack: Up until the 1960s, *applejack* was the term for apple brandy produced by freeze distillation, which was colloquially referred to as *jacking*. In this process, barrels of fermented cider were left outside during the winter. The water in the cider freezes and can be skimmed off, leaving a much more alcoholic liquid behind. This process results in an alcohol content of about 25 to 40 percent. More recently, *applejack* has come to legally mean a mixture of apple brandy and neutral spirit. The popularity of vodka led Laird's, a New Jersey–based company, to petition for the definition of *applejack* to be changed. Their work resulted in the current legal definition and in less intense, less appley products.

Calvados: By law, Calvados is an apple brandy made in the Lower Normandy region of France. It is distilled once or twice from a cider made from specially grown and chosen apples, which are divided into four types: bitter, sweet, bittersweet, and sour-acidic. The tradition of distilling cider is first mentioned in print in 1553, but Calvados was likely produced before then. After distillation, oak casks used for aging bring more spice to mature brandies, but younger iterations tend to have a stronger apple flavor. Several local designations exist including Pays d'Auge, which must be distilled twice and made in a specific area of the Calvados-producing region. One type of Calvados, labeled as Domfrontais, is made from 30 percent local pears. Like Cognac, its age is designated by star ratings and a series of designations starting at Fine and topping out at Extra, or XO.

Eaux-de-vie: These unaged fruit brandies are produced from everything except grapes. Strictly speaking, any unaged distilled spirit is an eau-de-vie, but in practice, the term is usually restricted to those made from fruit. They tend to be clear and are not sweetened before bottling, and they have been enjoyed as after-dinner drinks for a very long time. In the world of distilled spirits, they tend to be relatively low proof, clocking in around 40 to 43 percent ABV. Since they are unaged, they retain the character of their base ingredients, making a pour almost like biting into a ripe fruit.

Kirsch: Kirsch, or *kirschwasser*, is a fruit brandy made from sour morello cherries and their pits. It is made in Germany but also in Switzerland and the Alsace region of France. After it is distilled twice, it is typically allowed to mellow in earthenware vats. Most people will suggest it be drunk chilled from a spirits glass.

Similar Spirits

Grappa: Like brandy, Italian grappa is made from grapes. But grappa is produced from what is left behind after grapes are pressed to make wine—not from the wine itself. Called *pomace*, this leftover material includes the skins and husks of the grapes, and sometimes the stems. Over the past few years, grappa has undergone an almost-miraculous transformation, with producers focusing on quality rather than quantity. After distillation, some is aged for at least a year in oak, cherry, or ash barrels and called *invecchiata*.

Marc: This French product, very similar to grappa, is made from the pomace, called *marc* in the United States. It is usually lightly colored and is colloquially referred to as poor man's brandy or vintner's brandy. Style-wise, it can range from a light, delicate spirit to a stronger, more aromatic one. It is typically consumed as a digestif.

Brandy Tips

As with whiskey, some drinkers believe brandy is for sipping, not mixing. But these individuals ignore hundreds of years of cocktail history. Fruit is available in most places, which has meant that liquor distilled from fruit is as well.

Younger blends of grape-based brandies, such as VS Cognacs, are best in bold punches. To add a bit more nuance to cocktails, reach for a VSOP for its longer time in the barrel. Older brandies and XO Cognacs are best saved for sipping, since some parts of them may date from beyond your lifetime. But as with all other spirits, do not be scared to use an older spirit in a cocktail. Do consider saving it for a very, very special occasion.

When experimenting with creating new cocktails, note that brandy pairs well with fruit and baking spice flavors like cinnamon and nutmeg. Citrus is also tasty with it, either through fresh juices or orange liqueurs. Vermouths, herbal liqueurs, and other aromatic ingredients also pair well. Unfortunately, brandy does not play well with assertive or aggressive bitter liqueurs, so proceed with caution.

CLASSIC
BRANDY COCKTAILS

Brandy Alexander CREAMY
COCKTAIL GLASS | JIGGER, SHAKER, HAWTHORNE STRAINER

1 ounce brandy
1 ounce crème de cacao
1 ounce heavy cream

Shake all ingredients well with cracked ice. Strain into a chilled cocktail glass and serve.

Gin Alexander: *Substitute gin for brandy.*
Coffee Alexander: *Substitute coffee liqueur for crème de cacao.*

Brandy Crusta CITRUSY
COCKTAIL GLASS | KNIFE, JIGGER, SHAKER, HAWTHORNE STRAINER

Sugar rim (see page 49)
1 lemon twist (see page 49), for garnish
2 ounces Cognac
1 teaspoon orange Curaçao
½ teaspoon freshly squeezed lemon juice
1 dash Angostura bitters

Carefully curl the lemon peel around the inside of the chilled and rimmed cocktail glass. Shake all the remaining ingredients with ice, and strain into the cocktail glass. Add 1 ice cube and serve.

Bourbon Crusta: *Substitute bourbon for Cognac.*
Rum Crusta: *Substitute rum for Cognac.*

Milk Punch CREAMY
COLLINS GLASS | JIGGER, MIXING GLASS, BAR SPOON,
HAWTHORNE STRAINER

2 ounces brandy
½ ounce Simple Syrup (page 44)
6 to 8 ounces milk
Freshly grated nutmeg, for garnish (optional)

In a mixing glass, stir the liquid ingredients with ice to combine. Strain into a chilled Collins glass, sprinkle with nutmeg (if using), and serve.

Bull's Milk: *Substitute ½ ounce dark rum for ½ ounce brandy.*
Bourbon Milk Punch: *Substitute bourbon for brandy.*

Pisco Sour CITRUSY, CREAMY
COCKTAIL GLASS | JIGGER, SHAKER, HAWTHORNE STRAINER

1½ ounces pisco brandy
¾ ounce freshly squeezed lime juice
1 ounce Simple Syrup (page 44)
1 small egg white
3 drops Angostura bitters, for garnish

Shake all ingredients except the bitters without ice. Add ice and shake vigorously until chilled through, about 15 to 25 seconds. Strain into a chilled cocktail glass, garnish by dropping the bitters onto the foam, and serve.

Sidecar 1 CITRUSY
COCKTAIL GLASS | JIGGER, SHAKER, HAWTHORNE STRAINER

Sugar rim (page 49)
1½ ounces Cognac
¾ ounce Cointreau
¾ ounce freshly squeezed lemon juice

Shake all ingredients well with ice, strain into a chilled cocktail glass with a sugar rim, and serve.

Sidecar 2 CITRUSY
COCKTAIL GLASS | JIGGER, SHAKER, HAWTHORNE STRAINER

Sugar rim (page 49)
1 ounce Cognac
1 ounce Cointreau
1 ounce freshly squeezed lemon juice

Shake all ingredients well with ice, strain into a chilled cocktail glass with a sugared rim, and serve.

Tijuana Taxi: *Substitute tequila for brandy.*
Boston Sidecar: *Substitute light rum for Cognac.*
Bourbon Sidecar: *Substitute bourbon for Cognac.*

Stinger (also called a Judge) MINTY, STRONG

COCKTAIL GLASS | JIGGER, SHAKER, HAWTHORNE STRAINER

2¼ ounces brandy
¾ ounce white crème de menthe
2 short straws for garnish (optional)

Shake both ingredients well with cracked ice and strain into a chilled cocktail glass. Garnish with a pair of short straws (if using), and serve.

Brant: *Add 2 dashes Angostura bitters and garnish with a lemon peel.*
Picador: *Substitute light rum for brandy.*
White Spider: *Substitute vodka for brandy.*

CRAFT
BRANDY COCKTAILS

Alabazam CITRUSY, SPICY
COUPE OR COCKTAIL GLASS | JIGGER, SHAKER, HAWTHORNE STRAINER

1½ ounces Cognac
½ ounce Cointreau
¼ ounce Angostura bitters
¼ ounce freshly squeezed lemon juice
¼ ounce Simple Syrup (page 44)

Shake all ingredients well with ice, strain into a chilled coupe or cocktail glass, and serve.

Always Crashing the Same Car STRONG
Colin Shearn, Franklin Mortgage & Investment Company, Philadelphia

COCKTAIL GLASS | KNIFE, JIGGER, MIXING GLASS, BAR SPOON, HAWTHORNE STRAINER

1½ ounces 100 proof apple brandy, preferably
  Laird's Apple Brandy
1½ ounces Bonal Gentiane-Quina Aperitif
1 teaspoon green Chartreuse
1 to 2 dashes aromatic bitters
1 grapefruit peel twist (see page 49), for garnish

Add all liquid ingredients to a mixing glass and fill the glass halfway with ice. Stir vigorously, and strain into a chilled cocktail glass. Twist the oils from a grapefruit twist over the drink, discard the peel, and serve.

Applejack Rabbit CITRUSY
COUPE GLASS | JIGGER, SHAKER, HAWTHORNE STRAINER

2 ounces 100 proof apple brandy, preferably Laird's Apple Brandy
¾ ounce freshly squeezed lemon juice
¾ ounce freshly squeezed orange juice
½ ounce maple syrup, preferably Deep Mountain Grade B

Shake all ingredients well with ice, strain into a chilled coupe, and serve.

B&B STRONG
ROCKS GLASS | JIGGER, MIXING GLASS, BAR SPOON, JULEP STRAINER

1 ounce brandy
1 ounce Bénédictine

In a mixing glass, stir both ingredients well with ice, strain into a chilled rocks glass, and serve.

Banana Cognac STRONG
Bryant Jane, Velveteen Rabbit, Las Vegas

SNIFTER | JIGGER, MIXING GLASS, BAR SPOON, HAWTHORNE STRAINER

1 ounce Cognac, preferably Maison Rouge
¾ ounce banana liqueur, preferably Giffard
½ ounce crème de cacao
¼ ounce Fernet Branca
1 banana chip, for garnish

In a mixing glass, stir all liquid ingredients well with ice. Strain into a chilled snifter, garnish with a banana chip, and serve.

Black Jack STRONG

 Interpreted by Jim Meehan, New York City

COUPE GLASS | JIGGER, SHAKER, HAWTHORNE STRAINER

1½ ounces Pierre Ferrand Ambre Cognac
½ ounce Clear Creek Kirschwasser
½ ounce coffee concentrate*
¼ ounce Demerara Syrup (page 44)
3 cherries on a pick, for garnish

Shake all liquid ingredients with ice. Strain into a chilled coupe glass, garnish with 3 cherries on a pick, and serve.

Coffee concentrate should be available at your local grocery store, but it is also easy to make from scratch.

Coffee Concentrate: In a 40-ounce glass jar, combine 1 cup ground coffee beans with 4 cups water. Stir, and let sit overnight.

Brandy Snapper CITRUSY, FRUITY

HIGHBALL GLASS OR COLLINS GLASS | KNIFE, JIGGER, SHAKER, HAWTHORNE STRAINER

2 ounces Cognac
½ ounce freshly squeezed lemon juice
½ ounce Honey Syrup (page 44)
1 teaspoon crème de framboise
½ orange wheel (see page 49), for garnish

Shake all liquid ingredients well with ice until chilled. Strain into a chilled highball glass or Collins glass filled with cracked ice, garnish with the orange wheel, and serve.

Chicago BUBBLY, STRONG
CHAMPAGNE FLUTE | JIGGER, MIXING GLASS, BAR SPOON,
HAWTHORNE STRAINER

Sugar rim (see page 49)
2 ounces brandy
1 dash Cointreau
1 dash Angostura bitters
Sparkling wine, for topping

In a mixing glass, stir all ingredients except the sparkling wine
well with ice. Strain into a chilled champagne flute with a
sugared rim, top with sparkling wine, and serve.

Coffee Cocktail COFFEE, CREAMY
ROCKS GLASS | JIGGER, SHAKER, HAWTHORNE STRAINER,
FINE STRAINER

2 ounces tawny port
1 ounce Cognac
½ ounce Simple Syrup (page 44)
1 whole egg
Freshly grated nutmeg, for garnish

Shake all ingredients except the nutmeg with ice, and strain
into a chilled rocks glass. Garnish with a sprinkle of nutmeg,
and serve.

Corpse Reviver No. 1 STRONG
COUPE GLASS | JIGGER, MIXING GLASS, BAR SPOON, JULEP STRAINER

1 ounce Armagnac
1 ounce Calvados
1 ounce sweet vermouth
1 maraschino cherry, for garnish

In a mixing glass, stir all liquid ingredients well with ice.
Strain into a chilled coupe, garnish with the cherry, and serve.

Dulchin FRUITY
COCKTAIL GLASS | JIGGER, SHAKER, HAWTHORNE STRAINER

2 ounces pisco
1 ounce apricot eau-de-vie
1 ounce freshly squeezed lime juice
2 teaspoons Grand Marnier
1 teaspoon grenadine (store-bought or homemade, page 45)

Shake all ingredients with ice, strain into a chilled cocktail
glass, and serve.

East India Cocktail TROPICAL
COCKTAIL GLASS | KNIFE, JIGGER, MIXING GLASS, BAR SPOON,
HAWTHORNE STRAINER

2 ounces Cognac
1 teaspoon Curaçao
1 teaspoon pineapple syrup
2 dashes maraschino cherry liqueur
2 to 3 dashes Angostura or Peychaud's bitters
1 maraschino cherry, for garnish
1 flamed orange peel (see page 48), for garnish

In a mixing glass, stir all liquid ingredients well with
ice. Strain into a chilled cocktail glass. Garnish with the
maraschino cherry and orange peel, and serve.

Fort Washington Flip CREAMY

◀ *Misty Kalkofen, Boston*

COCKTAIL GLASS | JIGGER, SHAKER, HAWTHORNE STRAINER

1½ ounces Laird's Applejack
¾ ounce Bénédictine
½ ounce maple syrup
1 fresh egg
Freshly grated nutmeg, for garnish

Add the first 3 ingredients to a cocktail shaker, followed by
the egg. Shake vigorously without ice for 10 to 15 seconds. Add
ice, and shake vigorously for another 10 to 15 seconds. Strain
into a chilled cocktail glass, garnish with nutmeg, and serve.

Harvard Cocktail STRONG

COCKTAIL GLASS | JIGGER, MIXING GLASS, BAR SPOON,
HAWTHORNE STRAINER

1½ ounces Cognac
1 ounce sweet vermouth
2 or 3 dashes Angostura bitters
Soda, for topping

In a mixing glass, stir the first 3 ingredients well with cracked
ice. Strain into a chilled cocktail glass, and top with an ounce
or so of cold club soda or seltzer, and serve.

Jack Rose CITRUSY, APPLEY

COUPE GLASS | KNIFE, JIGGER, SHAKER, HAWTHORNE STRAINER

2 ounces 100 proof apple brandy, preferably Laird's Apple Brandy
¾ ounce grenadine (store-bought or homemade, page 45)
1 ounce freshly squeezed lemon juice
1 dash Peychaud's bitters
1 lemon twist (see page 49), for garnish

Shake all liquid ingredients well with ice until chilled, and strain into a chilled coupe glass. Twist the lemon peel over the surface, rub around the rim of the glass, and serve.

Japanese Cocktail STRONG

COCKTAIL GLASS | KNIFE, JIGGER, MIXING GLASS, BAR SPOON, HAWTHORNE STRAINER

2 ounces Cognac
½ ounce orgeat (store-bought or homemade, page 46)
3 dashes Angostura bitters
1 lemon twist (see page 49), for garnish

In a mixing glass, stir all liquid ingredients well with cracked ice. Strain into a chilled cocktail glass, garnish with a twist of lemon peel, and serve.

La Tour Eiffel STRONG

 Gary Regan, New York City

CHAMPAGNE FLUTE | KNIFE, JIGGER, MIXING GLASS, BAR SPOON, HAWTHORNE STRAINER

¼ ounce absinthe
2½ ounces XO Cognac
½ ounce Cointreau
½ ounce Suze gentian bitter liqueur
1 lemon twist (see page 49), for garnish

Pour the absinthe into a chilled champagne flute, tilting and rotating the glass to coat the interior. Add a few ice cubes. Pour the remaining liquid ingredients into an ice-filled mixing glass and stir. Discard the ice and any excess absinthe from the flute, and strain the drink into it. Garnish with the lemon twist, and serve.

Metropole STRONG

COCKTAIL GLASS | JIGGER, MIXING GLASS, BAR SPOON, HAWTHORNE STRAINER

1½ ounces Cognac
1½ ounces dry vermouth
2 dashes Peychaud's bitters
1 dash orange bitters (store-bought or homemade, page 40)
1 maraschino cherry, for garnish

In a mixing glass, stir all liquid ingredients well with cracked ice. Strain into a chilled cocktail glass, garnish with the cherry, and serve.

Morning Glory STRONG

ROCKS GLASS | KNIFE, JIGGER, MIXING GLASS, BAR SPOON, HAWTHORNE STRAINER

1 ounce rye whiskey

1 ounce Cognac

1 teaspoon orange Curaçao

1 teaspoon Simple Syrup (page 44)

2 dashes absinthe

2 dashes Angostura bitters

Club soda, for topping

1 lemon twist (page 49), for garnish

In a mixing glass, stir all but the last 2 ingredients well with ice. Strain into a chilled, ice-filled rocks glass, and top with 1 or 2 ounces of club soda, to taste. Twist the lemon peel over the drink, drop it in, and serve.

Northern Spy APPLEY

Josey Packard, Boston

CHAMPAGNE FLUTE | JIGGER, SHAKER, FINE STRAINER

1 ounce applejack

½ ounce nonalcoholic apple cider

¼ ounce freshly squeezed lemon juice

¼ ounce apricot liqueur

Sparkling wine, for topping

Shake all ingredients except the wine well with ice. Strain into a chilled champagne flute, top with sparkling wine, and serve.

Pink Panther FLORAL, CITRUSY

Yael Vengroff, New York, New York

COCKTAIL GLASS | JIGGER, SHAKER, MUDDLER,
HAWTHORNE STRAINER, FINE STRAINER

3 raspberries
2 ounces Capel Pisco brandy
¾ ounce freshly squeezed lemon juice
¾ ounce orgeat (store-bought or homemade, page 46)
4 drops rosewater
1 egg white

In a cocktail shaker, muddle the raspberries. Add the remaining ingredients, and shake without ice. Add ice, and shake again. Double strain into a chilled cocktail glass, and serve.

Saratoga STRONG

COCKTAIL GLASS | KNIFE, JIGGER, MIXING GLASS, BAR SPOON,
HAWTHORNE STRAINER

1 ounce brandy
1 ounce rye whiskey
1 ounce sweet vermouth
2 dashes Angostura bitters
1 orange twist (see page 49), for garnish

In a mixing glass, stir all liquid ingredients well with ice. Strain into a chilled cocktail glass, garnish with the orange twist, and serve.

BRANDY

Savoy Tango FRUITY, STRONG

COCKTAIL GLASS | JIGGER, MIXING GLASS, BAR SPOON,
HAWTHORNE STRAINER

1½ ounces sloe gin
1½ ounces apple brandy
1 maraschino cherry, for garnish

In a mixing glass, stir the liquid ingredients well with cracked
ice. Strain into a chilled cocktail glass, garnish with the
cherry, and serve.

Vieux Carré STRONG

ROCKS GLASS | JIGGER, MIXING GLASS, BAR SPOON,
HAWTHORNE STRAINER

¾ ounce rye whiskey
¾ ounce Cognac
¾ ounce sweet vermouth
1 bar spoon Bénédictine
2 dashes Peychaud's bitters
2 dashes Angostura bitters
1 maraschino cherry, for garnish

In a mixing glass, stir all liquid ingredients well with ice.
Strain into a chilled rocks glass filled with ice, garnish with
the cherry, and serve.

THE CLASSIC & CRAFT COCKTAIL RECIPE BOOK

Widow's Kiss STRONG
COCKTAIL GLASS | JIGGER, MIXING GLASS, BAR SPOON,
HAWTHORNE STRAINER

1½ ounces Calvados
¾ ounce yellow Chartreuse
¾ ounce Bénédictine
2 dashes Angostura bitters
1 maraschino cherry, for garnish

In a mixing glass, stir all liquid ingredients well with ice.
Strain into a chilled cocktail glass, garnish with the cherry,
and serve.

Yolanda STRONG
COCKTAIL GLASS | KNIFE, JIGGER, SHAKER, HAWTHORNE STRAINER

1 ounce sweet vermouth
¾ ounce Cognac
¾ ounce gin
1 dash absinthe
1 dash grenadine (store-bought or homemade, page 45)
1 lemon twist (see page 49), for garnish

Shake all liquid ingredients well with ice. Strain into a chilled
cocktail glass, garnish with the lemon twist, and serve.

CHAPTER FIVE

CHAMPAGNE & SPARKLING WINES

In much of the world, celebrations call for a glass of bubbly wine. Hailed by rappers like Kanye West, actors like Bette Davis, and writers like Oscar Wilde, the drink's reputation has remained unchanged for centuries. No matter the occasion, the luxury of a bubbly wine is usually appropriate. For many years, the name **champagne** referred to any sparkling wine, no matter its origin. But French producers in the Champagne region cried foul and set guidelines that required anything labeled as Champagne to be produced in that region. Today, true Champagnes are capitalized in print, whereas others are not.

CHAMPAGNE MUST BE CARBONATED by a specific process known as the *Méthode Champenoise*. However, in recent years, other sparklers have gained traction for sipping solo and mixing in cocktails, either for their quality or economy of price. As a result, many recipes call for sparkling wine rather than specifying one in particular. At home, the same is true. Though you can mix with expensive Champagnes if you so choose, there are other options available that will provide the same flavor and consistency for less money. But sometimes, it is worth it to splurge on the good stuff.

Types of Champagne

Champagne is typically classified by region and quality level, and labeled with its resulting sugar content. But the labels that designate these traits use terms that may be unfamiliar to most casual drinkers. A few of the words used in the champagne world do not mean the same thing they mean elsewhere. For example, vintage champagnes may be old, but they are produced only from a single year's grape crop. If a year is not listed, the bottle is considered nonvintage and is likely made from a blend of years. Nonvintage champagne is much more common and is often more expressive of a house's style. Further, three grapes, pinot noir, pinot meunier, and chardonnay, are the varietals primarily used for champagne. Each adds a different quality: Chardonnay gives acidity, pinot noir body, and pinot meunier the aroma.

Blanc de noirs: This term literally translates to "white from blacks" and refers to the champagnes made with pinot noir and pinot meunier grapes, two of the three principal grapes of champagne-making. These champagnes are much less common than blanc de blancs. Once the grapes are picked, they are gently pressed to prevent the skins from bleeding color into the resulting juice. After pressing, the remaining skins are quickly removed to prevent any further pigment transfer. These champagnes are more robust wines with richer body.

But depending on the ratio of pinot noir grapes to pinot meunier, the flavors can vary widely.

Blanc de blancs: Blanc de blanc champagnes are made only from white grapes, primarily chardonnay grapes. Generally, these wines are made in the Côte des Blancs and the Côte de Sézanne within the region of Champagne and tend to be lighter and drier than blanc de noirs. These wines tend to be slightly more similar than blanc de noirs, but the exact flavor profiles can range greatly depending on the soil type and the terroir. But keep in mind that a producer's style, that magical umbrella that includes everything from farming choices to blending techniques, has just as great of an effect on the wine's resulting flavor profile.

Rosé: Rosé champagnes gain their color from one of two processes. In one, the juice is pressed from a mixture of grapes and the skins are allowed to soak, adding color. This juice is blended with chardonnay wine. Other rosé champagnes are made by adding red wine to a finished champagne. The resulting drinks tend to have strong berry flavors from the red grapes or wine with the creamy, rich texture from the white.

Tête de cuvée: This type of champagne is usually assumed to be the pinnacle in luxury drinking. Bottles released less frequently as cuvée de prestige are considered to be the epitome of a winemaker's style. Usually, they are produced only in years where the grape crops from the premier vineyards are of exceptional quality. These wines are thought to be some of the best examples of *terroir*, or soil and Mother Nature's influence. They tend to hold up well to long-term holding, or cellaring. However, these champagnes are difficult to describe as a category because there are no legal requirements for their production, although they are treated as vintage wines. Their quality comes with a price: These champagnes tend to be more expensive—and sometimes, much more expensive—than a brand's nonvintage offerings. Only you can decide whether it is worth the extra cost for your table.

Dryness

Champagne and other sparkling wine is available in different levels of sweetness. Once the wine has gone through its second fermentation in the bottle, most of the remaining yeast is removed from the bottle through a process called *disgorgement*. At this point, a mixture of reserve wine and cane sugar is added to sweeten the wine so it is ready to sell. This addition is called *dosage*, and the amount of residual sugar is indicated on the label by one of the following:

Brut nature, also called non-dosé, has between 0 and 3 grams of residual sugar and no added dosage.

Extra brut can contain up to 6 grams of sugar.

Brut, the most common type of champagne, contains up to 12 grams of sugar per liter.

Extra sec, also called extra dry, contains between 12 and 20 grams of sugar per liter.

Sec, also labeled as dry, contains between 20 and 32 grams of sugar.

Demi-sec is relatively sweet and contains between 33 and 50 grams of sugars per liter.

Doux has largely fallen out of favor, though it was quite popular in the 1800s and before. It clocks in as the sweetest with more than 50 grams per liter.

Similar Spirits

Other sparkling wines from France can be found for much more reasonable prices. Crémant wines are produced in any French region other than Champagne and are labeled with the region. Where it is produced also determines the grapes used to make it, and it is a good substitute for champagne at a fraction of the cost.

THE CLASSIC & CRAFT COCKTAIL RECIPE BOOK

Blanquette de Limoux: Hailing from Limoux, this is one of the oldest sparkling wine–producing regions in France. It is made from Mauzac grapes with several different carbonation methods, but typically the Méthode Champenoise. Crémant made in the region typically features chardonnay and Chenin Blanc grapes.

Prosecco: This Italian sparkler is made from the Glera grape and tends to be simpler in flavor than Champagne. Perhaps for this reason, it is also largely considered to be America's favorite sparkling wine. The bubbles come not from the Méthode Champenoise but from a different secondary fermentation style known as the Charmat method. In this process, the secondary fermentation occurs before bottling, resulting in a wine that tends to be drier and fruitier than most champagne. Flavor-wise, proseccos often have notes of pear, apple, and delicate white flower. Most prosecco is usually extra dry, meaning that a small amount of sugar is added to it before it is bottled.

Cava: Typically made in the Méthode Champenoise in Spain, many of these sparkling wines are aged for longer than most Champagnes. Though many grape varietals can be used, the most common are Xarello, Parellada, and Macabeo. Historically, the Spanish sparkling wines exported to the United States have not been the best, but the quality of available cavas has exponentially increased in the recent past.

Sekt: Sekt encompasses virtually any sparkling wine produced in Germany. Due to the broad definition, the low-quality sekts have come to define the category. Look for Riesling-based sekts: These often have all the characteristics of Riesling, but with bubbles.

American sparkling wine: Within the United States, there are no laws governing what grapes can be used in which wines. Chardonnay and pinot noir grapes are most commonly used, and some American sparkling wines are made with the Méthode Champenoise, while others are not. Some United States wines rival the quality of true Champagne, especially from Oregon's cool climate. Thanks to variances in climate in winemaking regions and lack of regulation, the quality and distinctive characteristics of American sparkling wine differs so much as to render a defining national style impossible.

Champagne Tips

Champagne should be served chilled, but not too cold. Roughly the same guidelines can be applied to other sparkling wines, but when it comes down to it, drink it how you like it. It should be served at around 50 degrees, not at room temperature or ice cold. Lower-quality champagne should be served slightly warmer than refrigerator temperature, and higher-quality, older bottles should be served just a touch warmer. Ice buckets work for the original chilling but should be used for no more than about 20 minutes, or you can cool it in the fridge for 3 or 4 hours. When you are pouring the bubbly stuff by itself, skip the coupe glass: The shallow bowl warms much more quickly than a champagne flute. Further, the carbonation dissipates much more quickly in the coupe glass, and much of the flavor along with it. Once it is in the glass, do not swirl it as you would with most other wines. This, too, will allow the carbonation to escape. Do not decant it, as the increased exposure to oxygen will have the same effect as drinking out of a coupe. To fancify your presentation, consider sabering the bottle if you are adventurous. Only practice makes perfect with a sabre or knife, but there are plenty of YouTube tutorials available to help you figure it out.

To taste champagne or sparkling wine, smell it first, and then take a sip large enough to roll around your mouth. Your brain will associate what it is experiencing with things you have tasted in the past. It takes a good amount of experience to describe the exact flavors you are tasting, so trust your brain. Many experts will suggest saying that a wine is friendly or unfriendly rather than good or bad, as it expresses your personal preferences without adding a value judgment to the product. But in the end, that is up to you too.

CLASSIC
CHAMPAGNE & SPARKLING
WINE COCKTAILS

Bellini FRUITY
CHAMPAGNE FLUTE

2 tablespoons peach purée
Prosecco, for topping

Pour the peach purée into a chilled champagne flute, top with chilled prosecco, and serve.

Rossini: *Substitute strawberry purée for peach purée.*

Champagne Cocktail BUBBLY, STRONG
CHAMPAGNE FLUTE | KNIFE

1 sugar cube
3 dashes Angostura bitters
Brut champagne
1 lemon twist (see page 49), for garnish

Place the sugar cube in a chilled champagne flute. Dash the bitters onto the cube, and fill the glass with brut champagne or other sparkling wine. Garnish with the lemon twist, and serve.

Casino Cocktail: *Substitute absinthe for bitters, and float 1 tablespoon of Cognac on top.*
Orange: *Substitute orange twist for lemon twist.*

French 75 DRY, BUBBLY

COLLINS GLASS OR CHAMPAGNE FLUTE | JIGGER, SHAKER,
HAWTHORNE STRAINER

2 ounces London dry gin
1 teaspoon superfine sugar
½ ounce freshly squeezed lemon juice
5 ounces brut champagne

Shake the first 3 ingredients well. Strain into a chilled Collins
glass half full of cracked ice, top with brut champagne, and
serve. For a modern twist, use a chilled champagne flute
rather than a Collins glass.

King's Peg: *Substitute brandy for gin.*
French 95: *Substitute bourbon for gin.*
Mexican 75: *Substitute tequila for gin.*

Kir Royale FRUITY, BUBBLY

CHAMPAGNE FLUTE

1 teaspoon crème de cassis
Champagne, for topping

Pour the cassis into a chilled champagne flute, top with
champagne, and serve.

Kir: *Substitute white wine for champagne.*

THE CLASSIC & CRAFT COCKTAIL RECIPE BOOK

Mimosa CITRUSY, BUBBLY
CHAMPAGNE FLUTE

4 ounces freshly squeezed orange juice
Brut champagne, for topping

Fill a chilled champagne flute two-thirds full of orange juice, top with brut champagne, and serve.

Grand Mimosa: *Add 1 tablespoon Grand Marnier.*
Buck's Fizz: *Add 1 tablespoon grenadine (store-bought or home-made, page 45), and reverse the measurements for orange juice and champagne.*

Seelbach STRONG, BUBBLY
CHAMPAGNE FLUTE | JIGGER, MIXING GLASS, BAR SPOON, HAWTHORNE STRAINER

1 ounce bourbon
½ ounce Cointreau
7 dashes Angostura bitters
7 dashes Peychaud's bitters
Champagne, for topping
1 lemon twist (see page 49), for garnish

In a mixing glass, stir the first 4 ingredients briefly over ice. Strain into a chilled flute, and top with champagne. Garnish with the lemon twist, and serve.

CHAMPAGNE & SPARKLING WINES

CRAFT
CHAMPAGNE & SPARKLING
WINE COCKTAILS

Airmail CITRUSY, BUBBLY
COLLINS GLASS | JIGGER, SHAKER

2 ounces golden rum
½ ounce freshly squeezed lime juice
1 teaspoon honey
Brut champagne, for topping

In a chilled cocktail shaker, thoroughly shake the first 3 ingredients with cracked ice. Pour unstrained into a chilled Collins glass, top with champagne, and serve.

American Royal Zephyr STRONG, BUBBLY
Damon Boelte, Grand Army, Brooklyn, New York

COUPE GLASS | JIGGER, MIXING GLASS, BAR SPOON,
HAWTHORNE STRAINER

1 ounce bourbon, preferably Old Grand-Dad Bonded
1 ounce Lillet Rosé
2 dashes Angostura bitters
2 dashes Peychaud's bitters
2 dashes orange bitters (store-bought or homemade, page 40)
3 ounces champagne, for topping
1 maraschino cherry, for garnish

In a mixing glass, stir all liquid ingredients except the champagne. Strain into a chilled coupe glass, and top with the champagne. Garnish with the cherry, and serve.

Aperol Spritz CITRUSY, BUBBLY
RED WINE GLASS OR ROCKS GLASS | KNIFE, JIGGER, BAR SPOON

3 ounces prosecco
2 ounces Aperol
1 splash soda
1 orange slice, for garnish

Add ice to a chilled red wine glass or rocks glass. Pour in all liquid ingredients, and stir gently. Garnish with an orange slice, and serve.

The Bitter End SPICY, BUBBLY
Adam Hodak, Green Russell Bar, Denver

CHAMPAGNE FLUTE | JIGGER, BAR SPOON

1 ounce Leopold whiskey
1 ounce ginger liqueur, preferably Domaine de Canton
Splash freshly squeezed lime juice, for topping
Prosecco, for topping
¼ ounce Fernet Branca, to float (see page 57)

Pour the whiskey and ginger liqueur into a chilled champagne flute, and top with the lime juice and prosecco. Float the Fernet on top to finish, and serve.

Campari Spritz CITRUSY, BITTER

RED WINE GLASS OR ROCKS GLASS | KNIFE, JIGGER, BAR SPOON

3 ounces prosecco
2 ounces Campari liqueur
1 splash soda
1 orange slice, for garnish

Add ice to a chilled red wine glass or rocks glass. Pour in all liquid ingredients, and stir gently. Garnish with the orange slice, and serve.

~~~~~~

Death in the Afternoon STRONG

CHAMPAGNE FLUTE | JIGGER, BAR SPOON

1 ounce absinthe
Champagne, for topping

Pour the absinthe into a chilled champagne glass. Top with champagne, stir to combine, and serve.

~~~~~~

Flirtini FRUITY

MARTINI GLASS | KNIFE, JIGGER, SHAKER, HAWTHORNE STRAINER

3 ounces pineapple juice
2 ounces vodka
½ ounce Triple Sec
Champagne, for topping
1 pineapple wedge, for garnish
1 maraschino cherry, for garnish

Shake the first 3 ingredients with ice until chilled. Strain into a chilled martini glass, and top with champagne. Garnish with the pineapple wedge and maraschino cherry, and serve.

THE CLASSIC & CRAFT COCKTAIL RECIPE BOOK

Oregon Orchard STRONG

 Jeremy Mielen, Tasty n Alder, Portland, Oregon

CHAMPAGNE FLUTE | JIGGER, MIXING GLASS, BAR SPOON, HAWTHORNE STRAINER

2 dashes Regan's orange bitters
1 ounce Aria gin
½ ounce Rothman & Winter Orchard Apricot Liqueur
1 ounce verjus
Dry cava, for topping

In a mixing glass, stir all ingredients except the cava with ice. Strain into a chilled champagne flute, top with dry cava, and serve.

Prince of Wales FRUITY

COUPE GLASS | JIGGER, SHAKER, MUDDLER, HAWTHORNE STRAINER

1 (1-inch) cube of pineapple
¼ ounce Simple Syrup (page 44)
½ ounce freshly squeezed lemon juice
1 teaspoon maraschino cherry liqueur
1½ ounces rye whiskey
Champagne, for topping
1 lemon twist (see page 49), for garnish

In a cocktail shaker, muddle the first 5 ingredients. Add ice and shake well. Strain into a chilled coupe, and top with champagne. Garnish with the lemon twist and serve.

CHAMPAGNE & SPARKLING WINES

Sidecar 75 CITRUSY, BUBBLY

Jonas Anderson, Strøm Bar, Copenhagen, Denmark

COUPE GLASS | JIGGER, SHAKER, HAWTHORNE STRAINER

2½ ounces Cognac, preferably Merlet
½ ounce Triple Sec, preferably Merlet Trois Citrus
½ ounce champagne syrup*
¾ ounce freshly squeezed lemon juice
1 lemon peel or pickled pear slice for garnish (optional)

Shake all liquid ingredients with ice until chilled through. Strain into a chilled coupe glass, garnish with a lemon peel or slice of pickled pear (if using), and serve.

To make the champagne syrup, mix 3 cups sugar for every 2 cups flat champagne. Stir until the sugar is dissolved, but do not heat.

That's Probably Him STRONG

Jimmy Hibbard, Barrelhouse Flat, Chicago

CHAMPAGNE FLUTE | JIGGER, MIXING GLASS, BAR SPOON, HAWTHORNE STRAINER

1 ounce gin, preferably Plymouth
½ ounce Dolin dry vermouth
½ ounce Cocchi Rosa
¼ ounce apricot liqueur, preferably Rothman & Winter Orchard
  Apricot Liqueur
⅛ ounce freshly squeezed lemon juice
Sparkling wine, for topping

In a mixing glass, stir all ingredients except the sparkling wine with ice until chilled. Strain into a chilled champagne flute, top with the sparkling wine, and serve.

CHAPTER SIX

GIN

Shrouded in myth and half-truths, gin has long been a contentious spirit. Most people either love it or hate it, but seldom will you find someone with truly neutral feelings about it. Despite its notoriety, it is considered by many modern bartenders to be one of the most versatile liquors. Historically, it was the most popular clear liquor until the 1960s, when vodka sales overtook it.

THE MOST SIMPLISTIC WAY to describe gin is as a juniper-flavored vodka. Though this is not always true in practice, most gin producers do not make their own base spirit but instead infuse or steep their botanicals in neutral liquor produced elsewhere. The only hard-and-fast rule of gin production in the United States is that it must contain juniper.

Juniper has been used for centuries as a culinary and apothecary ingredient. This ingredient gives gins their traditional piney taste. Before it was used in gin, it was likely used to mask the unpleasant taste of other types of substandard booze. But juniper rarely appears by itself. Most gins are made from brand-specific blends of botanicals that account for the diversity within the category.

Descended from the Dutch spirit genever, gin is a traditionally British liquor that has been adopted and produced all over the world since its creation. Gin production blossomed for the first time during the reign of Dutch king William of Orange. With restrictive tariffs on French brandy, English gin became popular, especially in a network of dram shops called gin joints. The inexpensive spirits sold at these establishments became popular with members of the lower class and were blamed for the social ills of the time. In response to the Gin Craze, British laws were changed to try to curb the disorderly conduct caused by gin-drinking citizens. Gin joints started serving beer and wine as well, leading to the precursors of modern bars.

Over time, famous drinkers, including F. Scott Fitzgerald, W. C. Fields, and Franklin D. Roosevelt, have chosen gin over most other tipples, and they partook frequently.

The readily available styles of gin have evolved over the years, a development that brings diversity to the market—and makes matching styles with cocktails a bit more challenging. When a recipe calls simply for gin, rely on your best judgment—and general stylistic differences. Though discovering exact differences between the categories will require many rounds of martinis or gin and tonics, this research is often what makes the world of cocktails so much fun.

THE CLASSIC & CRAFT COCKTAIL RECIPE BOOK

Types of Gin

London dry gin: London dry gin is arguably the most recognizable type of gin. It has an intense juniper-forward flavor and is usually made from a neutral grain base. If modern cocktails do not specify a type, you can usually use your favorite London dry. It is a relative newcomer to the gin world, having originated in the 1820s and risen to popularity in the 1880s. Beefeater and Tanqueray are probably the most recognizable brands, though many other newcomers are coming onto the market every year. Despite the name, the legal definition does not require it to be made in a certain place.

Navy proof: Technically, navy-proof gin is not a legally defined category. But like cask-strength or barrel-proof whiskies, the term designates a high-proof liquor. As the story goes, drunk sailors spilled their gin or rum onto the gun powder. To make sure it would be usable during battle, they stocked high-proof alcohol on ships. It must be at least 57 percent alcohol by volume. However, it is unclear whether the backstory is true. We must note that most modern gins are tamer, proof-wise, than their predecessors, so there may be some validity to it after all.

Old Tom: Old Tom gins tend to be slightly sweet and lightly botanical, and it may be the missing link between genever and London dry gin. The added sugar balances the gin's flavor and smooths out some of the burn from its alcohol content, a practice well known to vodka makers. Its name is thought to have originated at bars that furtively doubled as gin dispensaries. Legend has it that the doors of these bars were emblazoned with a black tom cat and had a slot where drinkers could pay and receive a shot of gin. Possibly because of its bad reputation, this style was wildly popular during the nineteenth century but was extinct by the 1960s. During the craft cocktail renaissance, this style was rediscovered by bartenders and cocktail geeks trying to track down ingredients. Though it is now made by brands such as Hayman's and Ransom, it is still relatively rare. Old Tom gin works quite well in a Martinez (page 132) or Tom Collins (page 120).

113

Plymouth style: In truth, the only difference between Plymouth and London dry is that Plymouth must be made in the British city of the same name. It tends to be slightly earthier and less dry than London dry, and it is currently produced by only one brand: Plymouth.

New wave: A new style has recently emerged that is not geographically or legally defined. Usually made by newer distillers, such as Hendrick's, these tend to emphasize botanicals, citrus, or other flavors rather than juniper. Made around the world, gins that fall into this category vary from delicate, lightly flavored hooch to juniper-forward London dry–style gins. Though this category is more of an umbrella than an exact style, some products are labeled as "American dry gin," "New American," or "New Western."

Grape-based gin: Though most gin is made from neutral grain spirits, some is made from grape-based liquor. In terms of its character, this gin tends to be rounder with a fuller texture. One Spanish grape-based gin, Xoriguer, is the only type of gin other than Plymouth that has a legally defined geographical designation. These gins are delicious in a Gin and Tonic (page 117), which is insanely popular in Spain. G'Vine is another grape-based gin.

Barrel-aged gin: Barrel aging gin is not a new practice, but until recently, these products were not widely available in the United States. Flavor-wise, these usually have a mellower juniper flavor from their time in the barrel, tempered with a vanilla and caramel flavor and a maltiness that is more familiar in whiskies than gins. These tend to be a bit more expensive, but products like Ransom and Martin Miller's take the Ramos Gin Fizz (page 136), Tom Collins (page 120), and other cocktails to a whole new level.

Similar Spirits

Genever: Genever is almost—but not quite—like gin. It is produced from a base of malt wine, making it richer and heavier than its gin counterparts, but it still has strong juniper notes. Up until the craft cocktail movement, it was rare to see it on a bar's shelves in the United States. It was an integral part of the early cocktail movement and is the basis for many enduring recipes. Stylistically, some genevers have not changed much over the years. Substitute it for gin in cocktails, or try some of the nineteenth-century genever cocktails.

Flavored Gin

As with vodka, some gin producers have branched out into making flavored versions of their primary product. Examples include almond gin, apple gin, lemon gin, and, most notably, sloe gin.

Sloe gin: Sloe gin is a liqueur made by flavoring gin with blackthorn berries, which are nicknamed sloe berries. The blackthorn fruit is unfamiliar to many because it is not cultivated, as it tastes terrible on its own. Soaking the berries in navy-strength gin with a bit of sugar results in a rich, tart liqueur. Traditionally, sloe gin was a British winter drink, but Americans paired it with citrus to create the Sloe Gin Fizz (page 139), the most famous sloe gin cocktail. Like many other traditional liqueurs, it was difficult to find a quality sloe gin until recently. Plymouth makes a delicious one.

Gin Tips

The range of botanicals and other flavors in gin make it the perfect liquor to mix with just about anything. Unlike vodkas, premium gins are rare, and a $20 bottle of a London dry like Broker's, Seagram's, or New Amsterdam will work well for most cocktails. Pairing the perfect gins with cocktails is a bit more complex. If in doubt, start with the three most common categories, London dry, Old Tom, and contemporary, and work your way out.

Some gins are quite sippable, but finding mixing gin is much easier. To craft the perfect gin and tonic or martini, experiment with Plymouth or different London dry gins or invest in a slightly more expensive premium bottle. You also may have heard—or talked about—bruising gin by shaking a martini. Though shaking and stirring do affect cocktails differently (see page 56), *bruising* is an ambiguous term that has almost no meaning. However you prefer your martini, from ingredients to how it is mixed, is a matter personal preference, not correctness.

Some people advise storing gin in the freezer. However, as with whiskey, chilling it completely changes its flavor and smell, and not always for the best. Keeping and mixing it at room temperature will also give you a better understanding of how long something needs to be shaken or stirred so it is perfectly diluted every time. But as with all things in cocktails, this too is based on your own personal preference. Make it how you like it.

THE CLASSIC & CRAFT COCKTAIL RECIPE BOOK

CLASSIC
GIN COCKTAILS

Gimlet CITRUSY
COUPE GLASS | KNIFE, JIGGER, SHAKER, HAWTHORNE STRAINER

2 ounces gin
1 ounce freshly squeezed lime juice
1 ounce Simple Syrup (page 44)
1 cucumber wheel (see page 49) or lime wedge, for garnish

Shake all liquid ingredients well with ice. Strain into a chilled coupe glass, garnish with a cucumber wheel or lime wedge, and serve.

Vodka Gimlet: *Substitute vodka for gin.*
Southside: *Gently muddle 6 to 8 fresh mint leaves with all ingredients and prepare.*

Gin and Tonic EARTHY, BITTER
ROCKS GLASS | KNIFE, JIGGER

2 ounces good gin
4 ounces chilled tonic water
1 or 2 lime wedges

Pour the gin and tonic into a chilled rocks glass full of ice. Garnish with the lime wedge(s), and serve.

Vodka and Tonic: *Substitute vodka for gin.*

Gin Smash CITRUSY

ROCKS GLASS | JIGGER, MUDDLER, SHAKER, HAWTHORNE STRAINER

1 fresh mint sprig, plus 1 more for garnish
¾ ounce Simple Syrup (page 44)
½ ounce freshly squeezed lemon juice
2 ounces gin

In a cocktail shaker, muddle 1 of the mint sprigs with the
Simple Syrup and lemon juice. Add the gin and ice. Shake and
strain the mixture into a chilled rocks glass filled with ice,
garnish with the other sprig of mint, and serve.

Brandy Smash: *Substitute brandy for gin.*
Whiskey Smash: *Substitute whiskey for gin.*

Martini DRY

COCKTAIL GLASS OR MARTINI GLASS | JIGGER, MIXING GLASS,
BAR SPOON, JULEP STRAINER OR HAWTHORNE STRAINER

1 ounce dry vermouth
2 ounces gin
1 olive, for garnish

In a mixing glass, stir the liquid ingredients with ice until
chilled through. Strain into a chilled cocktail or martini glass,
garnish with the olive, and serve.

Dry Martini: *Use ¼ to ½ ounce dry vermouth, to taste.*
Gibson: *Substitute a cocktail onion for the olive.*
Vodka Martini: *Substitute vodka for gin.*
Perfect Martini: *Substitute ½ ounce sweet vermouth for ½ ounce
dry vermouth.*
Dirty Martini: *Add a dash of olive brine.*
Upside-Down Martini: *Use 2 ounces dry vermouth and
1 ounce gin.*

Classic Negroni BITTER, CITRUSY
COCKTAIL GLASS | JIGGER, KNIFE, MIXING GLASS, BAR SPOON,
HAWTHORNE STRAINER

1 ounce gin
1 ounce sweet vermouth
1 ounce Campari liqueur
1 orange peel, for garnish

In a mixing glass, stir all liquid ingredients well with ice.
Strain into a chilled cocktail glass, garnish with the orange
peel, and serve.

Modern Negroni BITTER, CITRUSY
COCKTAIL GLASS | KNIFE, JIGGER, MIXING GLASS, BAR SPOON,
HAWTHORNE STRAINER

1½ ounces gin
1 ounce sweet vermouth
½ ounce Campari liqueur
1 orange peel, for garnish

In a mixing glass, stir all liquid ingredients well with ice.
Strain into a chilled cocktail glass, garnish with the orange
peel, and serve.

Boulevardier: *Substitute whiskey for gin.*
Rosita: *Substitute tequila for gin.*
Negroni Sbagliato: *Substitute prosecco for gin.*

Tom Collins CITRUSY, BUBBLY
COLLINS GLASS | KNIFE, JIGGER, BAR SPOON

2 ounces London dry gin
1 ounce simple syrup
1 ounce freshly squeezed lemon juice
Soda water, for topping
1 lemon wheel (see page 49), for garnish
Straw

Pour the first 3 ingredients into a chilled Collins glass
three-quarters full of cracked ice. Stir briefly, top with soda
water, garnish with the lemon wheel, and serve with a straw.

Rum Collins: *Substitute white rum for gin.*
Charlie Collins: *Substitute Jamaica rum for gin.*
John Collins: *Substitute whiskey for gin.*

CRAFT
GIN COCKTAILS

Abbey Cocktail CITRUSY
COCKTAIL GLASS | JIGGER, SHAKER, HAWTHORNE STRAINER

2 ounces gin
1½ ounces freshly squeezed orange juice
2 dashes orange bitters (store-bought or homemade, page 40)
1 maraschino cherry, for garnish

Shake all liquid ingredients well with ice, and strain into a
chilled cocktail glass. Garnish with the cherry, and serve.

Army and Navy CITRUSY, STRONG
COUPE GLASS | JIGGER, SHAKER, HAWTHORNE STRAINER

2 ounces London dry gin
¾ ounce freshly squeezed lemon juice
¾ ounce orgeat (store-bought or homemade, page 46)
2 dashes Angostura bitters
1 or 2 maraschino cherries

Shake all liquid ingredients well with ice, and strain into a
chilled coupe glass. Garnish with a maraschino cherry or two,
and serve.

Aviation CITRUSY, HERBAL
COCKTAIL GLASS | JIGGER, SHAKER, HAWTHORNE STRAINER

2 ounces gin
½ ounce maraschino cherry liqueur
¼ ounce crème de violette
¾ ounce freshly squeezed lemon juice
1 maraschino cherry, for garnish

Shake all liquid ingredients well, and strain into a chilled cocktail glass. Garnish with a cherry, and serve.

Bee's Knees
(also called the Honey Bee) CITRUSY

COUPE GLASS | JIGGER, SHAKER, HAWTHORNE STRAINER

1 ounce freshly squeezed lemon juice
1 ounce Honey Syrup (page 44)
2 ounces gin

Shake all ingredients well with ice, strain into a chilled coupe glass, and serve.

Bella, Bella TART
COCKTAIL GLASS | KNIFE, JIGGER, SHAKER, HAWTHORNE STRAINER

1 ounce gin
⅔ ounce Campari liqueur
½ ounce limoncello
½ ounce orange liqueur
⅔ ounce freshly squeezed orange juice
1 lime spiral (see page 49), for garnish

Shake all liquid ingredients well with ice, and strain into a chilled cocktail glass. Garnish with the lime spiral, and serve.

Boston Cocktail FRUITY, STRONG

COCKTAIL GLASS | JIGGER, SHAKER, HAWTHORNE STRAINER

¾ ounce dry gin
¾ ounce apricot nectar liqueur
¼ ounce grenadine (store-bought or homemade, page 45)
¼ ounce freshly squeezed lemon juice

Shake all ingredients well with ice, strain into a chilled cocktail glass, and serve.

Can't Dutch This HERBAL, CITRUSY

Kate Gerwin, Lüft Bar, Bismarck, North Dakota

COLLINS GLASS | JIGGER, SHAKER, HAWTHORNE STRAINER

1 ounce genever
½ ounce dry Curaçao
½ ounce Chinese 5-spice syrup
1½ ounces lemon sour
3 or 4 spice-infused mandarin orange sections,* for garnish

Shake all liquid ingredients well with ice, and strain into a chilled Collins glass full of crushed ice. Garnish with 3 or 4 spice-infused mandarin orange sections, and serve.

For spiced orange slices: Soak orange wedges in Chinese five-spice syrup for 2 to 4 hours.

Clover Club CITRUSY, CREAMY

COUPE GLASS | JIGGER, SHAKER, HAWTHORNE STRAINER

1½ ounces gin
¾ ounce freshly squeezed lemon juice
2 teaspoons raspberry syrup
1 egg white

Shake all ingredients vigorously without ice. Add ice and shake vigorously again for at least 10 seconds. Strain into a chilled coupe glass, and serve.

Corpse Reviver No. 2 CITRUSY, DRY

COCKTAIL GLASS | KNIFE, JIGGER, SHAKER, HAWTHORNE STRAINER

1 ounce gin
1 ounce Cocchi Americano Bianco or Lillet Blanc
1 ounce Cointreau
1 ounce freshly squeezed lemon juice
1 dash absinthe
1 orange peel, for garnish

Shake all liquid ingredients well with ice, and strain into a chilled cocktail glass. Garnish with the orange peel, and serve.

Dog Days TART, FIZZY
Charlie Moore, Knife, Dallas

COLLINS GLASS | JIGGER, SHAKER, MUDDLER, HAWTHORNE STRAINER, FINE STRAINER

½ ounce Honey Syrup (page 44)
2 strawberries, plus 1 more for garnish
1½ ounces Bulldog gin
¾ ounce Aperol
¾ ounce freshly squeezed lemon juice
2 ounces soda

In a cocktail shaker, muddle the Honey Syrup and 2 of the strawberries. Add the gin, Aperol, and lemon juice, and shake well with ice. Double strain into a chilled Collins glass, and top with soda and then ice. Garnish with the remaining strawberry, and serve.

THE CLASSIC & CRAFT COCKTAIL RECIPE BOOK

Dolomint HERBAL, CITRUSY
HIGHBALL GLASS | JIGGER

1 ounce gin
1 ounce Galliano
1 ounce freshly squeezed lime juice
Ginger ale, for topping
1 fresh mint sprig, for garnish

Pour the first 3 ingredients into a chilled highball glass filled
with ice. Top with ginger ale, garnish with a sprig of fresh
mint, and serve.

East Side CITRUSY, MINTY
COCKTAIL GLASS | KNIFE, JIGGER, MUDDLER, SHAKER,
HAWTHORNE STRAINER, FINE STRAINER

2 cucumber slices, plus 1 thin cucumber slice, for garnish
8 fresh mint leaves
2 ounces gin
1 ounce freshly squeezed lime juice
¾ ounce Simple Syrup (page 44)

In a cocktail shaker, lightly muddle the 2 cucumber slices
and the mint leaves. Add the liquid ingredients, and shake
well with ice. Strain into a chilled cocktail glass, float the thin
cucumber slice on top, and serve.

The Elvis TART, CITRUSY

 Beverly Johnson, Town, Carbondale, Colorado

ROCKS GLASS | KNIFE, JIGGER, SHAKER, HAWTHORNE STRAINER

3 ounces pink grapefruit juice
1½ ounces London dry gin
¼ ounce elderflower liqueur, preferably St-Germain
India pale ale, for topping
1 grapefruit twist (page 49), for garnish

In a cocktail shaker, combine the liquid ingredients except for
the beer. Add ice, and shake until the outside of the shaker
is frosty. Strain into a chilled rocks glass filled with ice, and
top with India pale ale. Garnish with the grapefruit twist,
and serve.

Flamingo FRUITY, CITRUSY

COCKTAIL GLASS | JIGGER, SHAKER, HAWTHORNE STRAINER

1 ounce gin
½ ounce apricot brandy
½ ounce freshly squeezed lime juice
¼ ounce grenadine (store-bought or homemade, page 45)

Shake all ingredients well with ice, strain into a chilled
cocktail glass, and serve.

Florida HERBAL, CITRUSY

COCKTAIL GLASS | JIGGER, SHAKER, HAWTHORNE STRAINER

¾ ounce gin
¼ ounce Triple sec
1 ounce freshly squeezed orange juice
1 teaspoon freshly squeezed lemon juice

Shake all ingredients with ice, strain into a chilled cocktail glass, and serve.

Foghorn SPICY, CITRUSY
ROCKS GLASS | KNIFE, JIGGER, BAR SPOON

2 ounces gin
½ ounce freshly squeezed lime juice
Ginger beer or ginger ale, for topping
1 lime wedge, for garnish
Short straw

Pour the gin and lime juice into a chilled rocks glass full of ice. Top with ginger beer, and stir gently. Garnish with a lime wedge, and serve with a straw.

Gin and Celery FRESH
Todd Smith and Erik Reichborn-Kjennerud, The Hideout at Dalva, San Francisco

ROCKS GLASS | KNIFE, JIGGER, SHAKER, HAWTHORNE STRAINER, FINE STRAINER

1½ ounces Hayman's Old Tom Gin
¾ ounce freshly squeezed lemon juice
½ ounce Small Hand Foods gum syrup
6 dashes celery bitters, plus 2 dashes for garnish
1 ounce Fever-Tree Tonic Water
1 lemon twist (page 49), for garnish

Shake the first 4 ingredients well with ice, and double strain into a chilled rocks glass. Add the Fever-Tree Tonic, and top with 2 dashes of bitters. Garnish with the lemon twist, and serve.

Gin Fizz CITRUSY, FRESH
HIGHBALL GLASS | JIGGER, SHAKER, HAWTHORNE STRAINER,
BAR SPOON

2 ounces gin
1 ounce freshly squeezed lemon juice
¾ ounce Simple Syrup (page 44)
2 to 3 ounces club soda, for topping

Shake the first 3 ingredients well with ice, and strain into a
chilled highball glass full of ice. Top with club soda, stir gently,
and serve.

Gin Rickey CITRUSY, BUBBLY
COLLINS GLASS | KNIFE, JIGGER

½ lime
2 ounces London dry gin
Splash Simple Syrup, optional (page 44)
Chilled club soda, for topping
1 lime wedge, for garnish

Squeeze lime juice into a chilled Collins glass full of ice. Toss
in the juiced shell, and add the gin and Simple Syrup (if using).
Top with club soda, garnish with a lime wedge, and serve.

Hanky Panky STRONG
COCKTAIL GLASS | KNIFE, JIGGER, MIXING GLASS, BAR SPOON,
HAWTHORNE STRAINER

1½ ounces gin
1½ ounces sweet vermouth
2 dashes Fernet Branca
1 orange peel, for garnish

In a mixing glass, stir all liquid ingredients well with ice. Strain into a chilled cocktail glass. Twist a small swath of orange peel over the surface of the drink, use it as a garnish, and serve.

Honolulu FRUITY

COCKTAIL GLASS | KNIFE, JIGGER, SHAKER, HAWTHORNE STRAINER

Sugar rim (see page 49)
2 ounces gin
½ ounce pineapple juice
½ ounce freshly squeezed orange juice
¼ ounce freshly squeezed lemon juice
¼ ounce Simple Syrup (page 44)
1 dash Angostura bitters
1 lemon wheel (see page 49), for garnish

Shake all liquid ingredients well with ice, and strain into a chilled cocktail glass with a sugared rim. Garnish with the lemon wheel, and serve.

Insanely Good Gin and Tonic HERBAL

Chaim Dauermann, Up & Up, New York City

COLLINS GLASS | KNIFE, JIGGER

1½ ounces Brooklyn Gin
½ ounce Suze gentian bitter liqueur
¼ ounce lime cordial or freshly squeezed lime juice
1 dash Angostura bitters
Q Tonic, for topping
1 lime wheel (see page 49), for garnish

Pour the first 3 ingredients into a chilled Collins glass, and follow with a dash of bitters. Top with ice and Q Tonic, garnish with the lime wheel, and serve.

Jasmine CITRUSY, BITTER
Paul Harrington, Spokane

COCKTAIL GLASS | KNIFE, JIGGER, SHAKER, HAWTHORNE STRAINER

1½ ounces gin
¾ ounce freshly squeezed lemon juice
¼ ounce Cointreau
⅛ ounce Campari liqueur
1 lemon twist (see page 49), for garnish

Shake all liquid ingredients well with ice. Strain into a chilled cocktail glass, garnish with a lemon twist, and serve.

Journalist STRONG
COCKTAIL GLASS | JIGGER, MIXING GLASS, BAR SPOON, HAWTHORNE STRAINER

2 ounces gin
½ ounce dry vermouth
½ ounce sweet vermouth
2 dashes freshly squeezed lemon juice
2 dashes Curaçao
1 dash Angostura bitters

In a mixing glass, stir all ingredients well with ice. Strain into a chilled cocktail glass and serve.

THE CLASSIC & CRAFT COCKTAIL RECIPE BOOK

Juliet and Romeo CITRUSY, MINTY

Toby Maloney, The Violet Hour, Chicago

COUPE GLASS | JIGGER, SHAKER, HAWTHORNE STRAINER

3 fresh cucumber slices
Tiny pinch salt
3 fresh mint sprigs, plus 1 fresh mint leaf for garnish
2 ounces gin
¾ ounce Simple Syrup (page 44)
¾ ounce freshly squeezed lime juice
3 drops rose water, plus 1 drop for garnish (optional)
3 drops Angostura bitters, plus 3 drops for garnish (optional)

In a cocktail shaker, muddle the cucumber with the salt. Add the mint, and gently push to the bottom of the shaker. Add all the liquid ingredients, and let sit for 30 seconds. Add ice, shake vigorously, and strain into a chilled coupe glass. Garnish with the mint leaf, place 1 drop of rose water on the mint leaf and 3 drops of bitters on the drink's surface, if desired, and serve.

Last Word HERBAL, CITRUSY

COUPE GLASS | KNIFE, JIGGER, SHAKER, HAWTHORNE STRAINER

¾ ounce gin
¾ ounce green Chartreuse
¾ ounce maraschino cherry liqueur
¾ ounce freshly squeezed lime juice
1 lime twist (see page 49), for garnish

Shake all liquid ingredients well with ice. Strain into a chilled coupe glass, garnish with a lime twist, and serve.

Maiden's Prayer CITRUSY

COCKTAIL GLASS | JIGGER, SHAKER, HAWTHORNE STRAINER

1½ ounces London dry gin
½ ounce Cointreau
½ ounce freshly squeezed lemon juice
½ ounce freshly squeezed orange juice

Shake all ingredients well with cracked ice, strain into a
chilled cocktail glass, and serve.

Martinez HERBAL

COCKTAIL GLASS | KNIFE, JIGGER, MIXING GLASS, BAR SPOON,
HAWTHORNE STRAINER

2 ounces Old Tom gin
1 ounce sweet vermouth
1 teaspoon maraschino cherry liqueur, preferably Luxardo
2 dashes orange bitters (store-bought or homemade, page 40)
1 strip lemon peel, for garnish

In a mixing glass, stir all liquid ingredients well with ice.
Strain into a chilled cocktail glass. Twist a strip of lemon peel
over the top, drop it in, and serve.

Mercy, Mercy FRESH, CITRUSY

 Joseph Schwartz, Little Branch, New York City

COCKTAIL GLASS | KNIFE, JIGGER, MIXING GLASS, BAR SPOON,
HAWTHORNE STRAINER

2 ounces gin
½ ounce Aperol
½ ounce Cocchi Americano
2 dashes Angostura bitters
1 orange twist, for garnish

Fill a mixing glass with ice, and add all the liquid ingredients.
Stir well, and strain into a chilled cocktail glass. Garnish with
the orange twist, and serve.

Moonshot SAVORY

ROCKS GLASS | JIGGER, MIXING GLASS, BAR SPOON,
HAWTHORNE STRAINER

3 ounces Clamato Tomato Cocktail
2 ounces gin
1 dash Tabasco Sauce

In a mixing glass, stir all ingredients well with ice. Strain into
a chilled rocks glass and serve.

Paradise Cocktail STRONG, CITRUSY

COCKTAIL GLASS | JIGGER, SHAKER, HAWTHORNE STRAINER

2 ounces London dry gin
½ ounce apricot brandy
1 ounce freshly squeezed orange juice
½ ounce freshly squeezed lemon juice

Shake all ingredients well with cracked ice, strain into a chilled cocktail glass, and serve.

Pegu Club CITRUSY, CREAMY

COCKTAIL GLASS | JIGGER, SHAKER, HAWTHORNE STRAINER

2 ounces gin
¾ ounce orange Curaçao or Grand Marnier
¾ ounce freshly squeezed lime juice
1 dash Angostura bitters
1 dash orange bitters (store-bought or homemade, page 40)

Shake all ingredients well with cracked ice, strain into a chilled cocktail glass, and serve.

Pimm's Cup FRUITY

HIGHBALL GLASS | KNIFE, JIGGER, MUDDLER

1 cucumber slice, plus 1 for garnish
5 or 6 fresh mint leaves, plus 1 for garnish
2 ounces Pimm's No. 1
3 ounces ginger beer or ginger ale

In a chilled highball glass, muddle the cucumber slice and mint leaves. Fill with ice. Add the Pimm's, and top with the ginger beer. Garnish with a cucumber slice and a mint leaf, and serve.

THE CLASSIC & CRAFT COCKTAIL RECIPE BOOK

Pink Gin BITTER, HERBAL
ROCKS GLASS | JIGGER, BAR SPOON

3 drops Angostura bitters
2 ounces Plymouth gin

Splash the bitters into a chilled rocks glass, and roll around to coat. Pour out the extra, pour in the gin, and add a couple of ice cubes. Stir, and serve.

Pink Lady FRUITY, HERBAL
COCKTAIL GLASS | JIGGER, SHAKER, HAWTHORNE STRAINER

1½ ounces London dry gin
½ ounce applejack
½ ounce freshly squeezed lemon juice
1 egg white
1 teaspoon grenadine (store-bought or homemade, page 45)
1 maraschino cherry, for garnish

Shake all liquid ingredients vigorously without ice. Add ice, and shake again. Strain into a chilled cocktail glass, garnish with the cherry, and serve.

Pliny's Tonic SPICY, FRESH
Bobby Heugel, Anvil Bar & Refuge, Houston

COCKTAIL GLASS | KNIFE, JIGGER, MUDDLER, SHAKER, HAWTHORNE STRAINER, FINE STRAINER

4 (½-inch) cucumber quarters
2 ounces habanero-infused Citadelle dry gin*
1 ounce freshly squeezed lime juice
¾ ounce Rich Simple Syrup (page 44)
5 fresh mint leaves

In the bottom of a cocktail shaker, muddle the cucumber quarters. Add the remaining ingredients. Shake well with ice and double strain into a chilled cocktail glass. Garnish with the mint leaves, and serve.

*Try a habanero infusion. See page 35 for more on the technique for infusing spirits with heat.

Ramos Gin Fizz CITRUSY, CREAMY
COLLINS GLASS | JIGGER, SHAKER, HAWTHORNE STRAINER, FINE STRAINER

1½ ounces gin
1 ounce heavy cream
1 tablespoon Simple Syrup (page 44)
½ ounce freshly squeezed lemon juice
½ ounce freshly squeezed lime juice
1 egg white (pasteurized, if you like)
3 drops orange flower water
1 ounce club soda, chilled, for topping

Shake all ingredients except the club soda vigorously without ice. Add ice, and shake again for at least 2 minutes (or longer, if you wish). Strain into a chilled Collins glass, top with club soda, and serve.

THE CLASSIC & CRAFT COCKTAIL RECIPE BOOK

Respect Your Elders HERBAL, FLORAL

Jonny Spielsinger, Seattle

ROCKS GLASS | KNIFE, JIGGER, SHAKER

1½ ounces gin
¾ ounce elderflower syrup
¾ ounce freshly squeezed lemon juice
1 dash lavender bitters, such as Scrappy's
1 lemon wedge and/or edible microflowers, for garnish

Shake all liquid ingredients well with ice, and pour unstrained into a chilled rocks glass. Garnish with a lemon wedge and/or microflowers, and serve.

Sawyer BITTER, STRONG

Don Lee, New York City

ROCKS GLASS | JIGGER, SHAKER, HAWTHORNE STRAINER

2 ounces gin
½ ounce freshly squeezed lime juice
½ ounce Simple Syrup (page 44)
14 dashes Angostura bitters
7 dashes Peychaud's bitters
7 dashes orange bitters (store-bought or homemade, page 40)
  or 4 dashes Regan's Orange Bitters No. 6 and 3 dashes
  Fee Brothers West Indian Orange Bitters

Shake all ingredients with ice. Strain into a chilled rocks glass and serve.

Sharpie Mustache BITTER

Sother Teague, Amor y Amargo, New York City

COCKTAIL GLASS | KNIFE, JIGGER, MIXING GLASS, BAR SPOON, HAWTHORNE STRAINER

¾ ounce Meletti amaro
¾ ounce Bonal Gentiane-Quina Aperitif
¾ ounce London dry gin
¾ ounce 100 proof rye whiskey
2 dashes Bittermens tiki bitters
1 orange twist (see page 49), for garnish

In a mixing glass, stir all liquid ingredients well with lots of ice. Strain into a chilled cocktail glass. Squeeze the orange twist over the drink, place it in the glass, and serve.

Silver Bullet CITRUSY, HERBAL

COCKTAIL GLASS | JIGGER, SHAKER, HAWTHORNE STRAINER

1½ ounces gin
½ ounce freshly squeezed lemon juice
½ ounce kümmel
1 teaspoon Simple Syrup (page 44), optional

Shake all ingredients well with ice, strain into a chilled cocktail glass, and serve.

Singapore Sling FRUITY

COLLINS GLASS | JIGGER, BAR SPOON

1 ounce London dry gin
1 ounce cherry liqueur, such as Cherry Heering
1 ounce Bénédictine
1 ounce freshly squeezed lime juice
2 ounces soda water, for topping
1 dash Angostura bitters, for topping

Pour the first 4 ingredients into a chilled Collins glass full of ice. Top with soda water, and stir briefly. Dash the Angostura bitters on top, and serve.

Sloe Gin Fizz FRUITY, CITRUSY

FIZZ GLASS OR COLLINS GLASS | JIGGER, SHAKER, HAWTHORNE STRAINER

¾ ounce sloe gin
¾ ounce gin
¾ ounce freshly squeezed lemon juice
½ ounce Simple Syrup (page 44)
1 egg white (optional)
Soda water, for topping

Shake all ingredients except the soda water. If using the egg white, shake without ice. Add ice, and shake until chilled through. Strain into a chilled fizz glass or Collins glass, top with soda, and serve.

Twentieth-Century Cocktail STRONG
COCKTAIL GLASS | KNIFE, JIGGER, SHAKER, HAWTHORNE STRAINER

1½ ounces gin
¾ ounce Lillet Blanc
¾ ounce freshly squeezed lemon juice
½ ounce white crème de cacao
1 lemon twist (see page 49), for garnish

Shake all liquid ingredients well with ice. Strain into a chilled cocktail glass, garnish with a lemon twist, and serve.

Vesper Martini DRY
COUPE GLASS | KNIFE, JIGGER, MIXING GLASS, BAR SPOON, HAWTHORNE STRAINER

3 ounces Plymouth gin
1 ounce premium vodka
½ ounce Lillet Blanc
1 lemon twist (see page 49), for garnish

Fill a mixing glass halfway with cracked ice. Add the liquid ingredients, and stir until chilled. Strain into a chilled coupe glass, garnish the top of the drink with a lemon twist, and serve.

THE CLASSIC & CRAFT COCKTAIL RECIPE BOOK

Who Dares Win CITRUSY, HERBAL

Mike Aikman, Edinburgh, Scotland

MARTINI GLASS | JIGGER, SHAKER, HAWTHORNE STRAINER,
FINE STRAINER

2 ounces Beefeater gin
¾ ounce freshly squeezed lemon juice
½ ounce orgeat (store-bought or homemade, page 46)
¼ ounce kümmel
Star anise, for garnish

Shake all liquid ingredients well with ice, and double strain
into a chilled martini glass. Garnish with star anise, and serve.

CHAPTER SEVEN

RUM

More often than not, rum, also known as **ron** or **rhum**, gets a bad rap. Somewhere between its piratical days and the fruity umbrella drinks of the more recent past, the spirit developed the reputation for being tropical, and not much else. Luckily, modern bartenders have explored the complexities of this undervalued spirit. The range in the category is larger than with almost any other aged liquor, thanks to generally loose laws governing production. The result is a spectrum of products that vary from vodka-like whites to ultra-aged, complex sippers.

ITS HISTORY IS ALMOST HARDER TO PIN DOWN than a singular description of rum. Sugarcane was introduced to the Caribbean by Christopher Columbus to fill demands from Europe for refined sugar. The refinement process produced a lot of molasses, which was considered waste rather than a tasty sweetener. Much of the excess was dumped into the ocean. At some point, someone noticed that molasses would ferment and decided to distill it into something more alcoholic. What came out of this experimentation was admittedly rough, harsh, and probably rather unpleasant. It is not difficult, then, to see why it gained its "kill-devil" nickname. At the time, its appeal was more to local drinkers looking for volume: Rum was cheap and plentiful. The spirit quickly caught on with sailors and was transported all over the world.

Rum took special root in the early American colonies. During the American Revolution, some of its appeal wore off as the flow of rum and molasses was cut off. Whiskey filled the void, and has largely done so ever since. But rum remained commonplace in many punch recipes, though its versatility in cocktails was not appreciated until many drinkers traveled abroad during Prohibition. During this time, modernist celebrities including Hemingway slunk off to Havana to vacation and drink and were ensnared by the spirit's charms. After Repeal, its reputation was boosted again by the invention of the pseudo-Polynesian tiki movement.

At its most basic, rum is a spirit distilled from sugarcane or sugarcane by-products, though the exact legal definitions that govern the spirit vary by country. Most countries require that rum is aged before it is bottled, but aging is not a universal requirement. Its flavor depends on several key factors, including the source of sugar, the yeast, how long it is fermented, how it is distilled, and how and where it is aged. Arguably, the type of sugar used for fermentation often has the biggest impact on flavor. In most countries, adding coloring or sugar before barreling or bottling is perfectly legal. Rum can be difficult to classify based on its country of origin, but we will try.

THE CLASSIC & CRAFT COCKTAIL RECIPE BOOK

Rum is made all over the world, but thanks to the breadth of the regulations, the resulting product varies widely. Many rums are labeled according to where they are made as well as their color or how long they are aged, so these classifications are examined below.

Caribbean islands: On the Caribbean islands, two main styles dominate. These are sometimes referred to as Spanish or French rums, depending on the country's primary colonial language. Spanish rum, or *ron*, is probably best typified by Cuban rum, a light, crisp style that is often paired with cigars. The French style, called *rhum*, is quite different. On the island of Martinique, this style is specifically known as *rhum agricole* and is made from freshly pressed sugarcane juice. During the Napoleonic Wars, the British blockaded the French. Since the French were not receiving sugar from their Caribbean colonies, scientists figured out how to make sugar from beets. Martinique was left with a surplus of sugarcane and began using fresh-pressed juice to make their rums. Generally, rhum tends to be higher proof and is available aged and unaged. It is distilled on whatever type of still is available. Taste-wise, this style tends to have fruitier and funkier flavors rather than the caramels of rum from other places.

Central America: As in the Caribbean, the styles of rum vary within Central America. Currently, the single Guatemalan rum producer works at a higher altitude to take advantage of the temperature changes to speed along aging. Here, the law requires that rum be made from filtered fresh cane juice that has been boiled down, giving it a bit of the depth of the rhum agricole. Outside of these, most countries tend to fall into the Spanish style outlined above.

South America: Most countries in South America make the lighter Spanish style, but a couple of countries have developed their own. For example, most Venezuelan rums tend to be lighter, but the country's regulations are some of the harshest in rum, requiring 2 years of aging. Guyana is home to demerara rum, a dark, rich style that tends to be more savory than sweet thanks to the less refined sugarcane slurry used to make it. The aged and overproof demerara rums tend to pop up in tiki recipes.

New England: Rum fueled the early colonies. New England had a thriving rum business as part of the triangular trade that fueled slavery and at the time produced a completely unique style. But the British naval blockade during the Revolutionary War made sugarcane much harder to import. New Englanders started drinking other spirits, especially whiskey, and local rum distilleries folded from lack of raw materials and customers. Recently, some distillers in the area have begun producing rum again, but it is not made in the colonial style.

Others: Rum is also made by some producers in Asia and Africa. However, rum from the Caribbean and Latin America is much more readily available. As a result, much of the rum from outside that region is not imported into the United States. Experts note that some regions in Africa are perfect for growing sugarcane and that we may see rum produced in those areas in the future. Right now, Starr African Rum in Mauritius distills molasses into a rum with a rich flavor. In the Philippines, Tanduay makes a rhum that is a bit spicier and bitterer than its counterparts from the Caribbean.

Light rum: Also labeled as blanco, silver, or white, light rum tends to be crisp, light bodied, and subtly flavored. Many believe that this rum is unaged, but it is actually aged for a short time and then filtered through charcoal to remove color. Usually, it is produced in a column still rather than a pot still, and it is used mainly for cocktails and infusions. Brand-wise, Bacardi makes the most recognizable white rum on the market. Other brands like Don Q purposefully process their rum so that it is almost as neutral as vodka, while others still are floral and fruity, like the Cuban Havana Club.

Gold rum: Gold rums tend to have stronger flavors than white and are also aged in oak barrels. Also labeled as *oro*, amber, or *ambre*, gold rums add more depth to cocktails than white, though some are colored with artificial additives rather than time in a barrel. Look for a mellow, fruity, slightly spicy blend in the El Dorado 12 year, or Don Q, an easy-to-mix blend of caramels and vanilla.

Dark rum: Dark rums are aged for a longer period than light or gold. These tend to be produced with pot stills and are sippable by themselves. Oftentimes, they are also used with other rums in traditional mai tais or as the base for funky cocktails usually made with whiskey. Taste-wise, their flavors range widely from dark chocolate and dried fruit to tobacco and molasses, but most are not as sweet as you might imagine. Pick up a Zaya 12 year for heavy, sweet vanilla or a Zacapa 23 for a bit more complexity.

Black rum: Though not necessarily aged for longer than the dark rums, black rums have some funk. These rums pair particularly well with ginger beer and bitters, so it is not surprising that Gosling's Black Seal works so wonderfully in a Dark 'n' Stormy (page 152) that they actually have the cocktail trademarked. For some funk, grab Cruzan Black Strap for a molasses-y, coffee-rich experience.

Flavored rum: As with vodka, rum makers have experimented with different flavors of rum. Typically, rum producers tend to stick with more tropical or spice flavors. It is not surprising, then, that the two most common commercially produced flavors are heavily sweetened spiced rum and coconut rum. For spiced rums, Captain Morgan and Sailor Jerry's both heavily feature vanilla, and cinnamon flavors and are frequently paired with Coca-Cola. Malibu, a coconut rum liqueur, is probably the most recognizable of the flavors and blends easily into a Piña Colada (page 163).

Naval rum: While not technically a type of rum, naval rum is a dark, full-bodied style made based on what was given to officers of the British navy in the bygone age. Usually, it is bottled at 100 proof or above.

Overproof: Technically, this term refers to rums that are over 120 proof, or 60 percent ABV. The best-known type is 151 rums, or rums sold at 151 proof. Like most spirits at that strength, they are not often drunk by themselves but are instead used for theatrical garnishes like flaming floats or to raise the alcohol content of other cocktails.

SIMILAR SPIRITS

Cachaça: Until 2013, the United States required cachaça to be labeled as rum, though it is now recognized to be a distinctly Brazilian product. Brazil's national spirit is distilled from sugarcane juice and is most similar to rhum agricole. It can be sold aged or unaged, must be bottled between 38 and 48 percent ABV, and is best known for its use in the Caipirinha (page 150). When it is aged, it often spends time in many different types of wood, but rarely in oak, rendering the resulting spirits distinctly different from their rum counterparts. Different classifications are based on how it is stored before bottling. These include *branca*, which has been stored in stainless steel and is either completely unaged or has been stored in colorless wood, and *amarela*, which is stored in wood but without aging requirements. Products labeled as aged cachaça must be made from at least 50 percent of a cachaça that has rested for at least 1 year in a barrel that is no more than 700 liters. Premium aged cachaça is aged for at least 1 year, and extra premium must be aged for at least 3—and both must contain only barrel-aged cachaça.

RUM TIPS

As with many other spirits, the craft cocktail boom caused a huge surge of interest in rums of all types. The huge variety within the genre lends itself well to all types of consumption, from straight sipping to mixing everything from spirituous drinks to complex, tropical tiki concoctions. Dark rums can be the best bet for sipping, but many people enjoy lighter varietals because they give a stronger sense of what goes into the spirit. By itself, rum is best served at room temperature like Cognac. As with brandy, your hand will warm the rum through the glass, releasing some of the aroma. Do not smell it as you would a wine: As with most spirits, the alcohol vapor can numb your sense of smell, making it harder to experience the full taste of the rum. For sipping, squatty fluted glasses like the Glencairn work well, as do brandy snifters.

For mixing, light and gold rums work very well in classics like the Daiquiri (page 151), but remember to steer clear of gold rums with artificial flavoring. Light rum especially can be substituted for vodka or tequila in almost any cocktail. Rhum agricole can bring funk to any of the classics but is often combined half and half with other rums to add depth and subtlety to cocktails. Likewise, dark rums—especially the less sweet varietals—can replace whiskey or brandy to add a whole new twist to older cocktails.

Cigars and rum are a natural pairing. They are produced in similar climates, with a similar level of craftsmanship. Usually, experts recommend a medium-bodied cigar to go with a dark rum, or one with some natural sweetness or creaminess to match a rum's style. But as with all things related to cocktails, it is something that is best suited to experimentation so that you can find the pairing that works with your palate.

CLASSIC
RUM COCKTAILS

Caipirinha CITRUSY
ROCKS GLASS | KNIFE, MUDDLER, JIGGER

½ lime
½ teaspoon sugar
2 ounces cachaça

Slice the lime into ½-inch rounds, cube them, and muddle in a chilled rocks glass with the sugar. Add a couple of ice cubes, pour in the cachaça, and serve.

Caipiroska: *Substitute vodka for cachaça.*

Cuba Libre CITRUSY, COLA
COLLINS GLASS | KNIFE, JIGGER, BAR SPOON

1 lime, halved
2 ounces dark rum
Cola-flavored soda, preferably Coca-Cola, for topping

Squeeze a lime into a chilled Collins glass, and add a couple of ice cubes. Pour in the rum, drop in one of the spent lime shells, and fill with the Coca-Cola. Stir briefly, and serve.

Mexicola: *Substitute tequila for rum.*

THE CLASSIC & CRAFT COCKTAIL RECIPE BOOK

Daiquiri CITRUSY

COCKTAIL GLASS | JIGGER, SHAKER, HAWTHORNE STRAINER

2 ounces white rum
¾ ounce Simple Syrup (page 44)
¾ ounce freshly squeezed lime juice

Shake all ingredients well with cracked ice, strain into a chilled cocktail glass, and serve. If you prefer dark rum, cut back on the Simple Syrup.

Bacardi Cocktail: *Use Bacardi rum, and add between 1 dash and 1 ounce grenadine (store-bought or homemade, page 45).*
Fruity Daiquiris: *Substitute fruit liqueurs for Simple Syrup.*
Ti' Punch: *Substitute rhum agricole for white rum.*

Hemingway Daiquiri TART

COCKTAIL GLASS | JIGGER, SHAKER, HAWTHORNE STRAINER

2 ounces white rum
¾ ounce freshly squeezed lime juice
½ ounce grapefruit juice
¼ ounce Simple Syrup (page 44)
1 teaspoon maraschino cherry liqueur

Shake all ingredients with ice, strain into a chilled cocktail glass, and serve.

Dark 'n' Stormy CITRUSY, GINGERY
COLLINS GLASS | JIGGER, BAR SPOON

2 ounces Gosling's Black Seal Rum
3 ounces ginger beer
½ ounce freshly squeezed lime juice
1 lime wedge, for garnish

Pour the first 3 ingredients into a chilled Collins glass full of
ice cubes. Stir gently to combine, garnish with the lime wedge,
and serve.

Hurricane FRUITY
HURRICANE GLASS | KNIFE, JIGGER, SHAKER, HAWTHORNE STRAINER

2 ounces dark rum
1 ounce passion fruit syrup
1 ounce freshly squeezed lemon juice
1 orange slice, for garnish
1 maraschino cherry, for garnish

Shake the first 3 ingredients well with ice, and strain into
a chilled hurricane glass filled with cubed or crushed ice.
Garnish with the orange slice and cherry, and serve.

THE CLASSIC & CRAFT COCKTAIL RECIPE BOOK

Mojito MINTY, CITRUSY
COLLINS GLASS | KNIFE, JIGGER, MUDDLER, BAR SPOON

3 fresh mint leaves
2 ounces white rum
½ ounce freshly squeezed lime juice
½ ounce Simple Syrup (page 44)
Club soda, for topping
1 lime wedge, for garnish
Stirring rod

In a chilled Collins glass, lightly press the mint leaves against the side of the glass. Fill the glass two-thirds full of cracked ice, and pour in rum, lime juice, and Simple Syrup. Top with club soda, garnish with the lime wedge and stirring rod, and serve.

Cojito: *Substitute 1 ounce coconut rum for 1 ounce white rum.*
Raspberry: *Add 4 or 5 raspberries to the mint leaves and press against the side of the glass. Garnish with extra raspberries.*

CRAFT
RUM COCKTAILS

Atlantic Breeze FRUITY
HIGHBALL GLASS | KNIFE, JIGGER

2 ounces cranberry juice
2 ounces pineapple juice
1½ ounces white rum
1 lime wedge, for garnish

Pour all liquid ingredients into a chilled highball glass, garnish with a lime wedge, and serve.

Batida FRUITY
HIGHBALL GLASS | JIGGER, SHAKER, HAWTHORNE STRAINER

2 ounces cachaça
1 ounce fruit purée
¾ ounce Simple Syrup (page 44)

Shake all ingredients with ice, strain into a chilled highball glass filled with ice, and serve.

THE CLASSIC & CRAFT COCKTAIL RECIPE BOOK

Bermuda Rum Swizzle FRUITY

ROCKS GLASS | KNIFE, JIGGER, SHAKER, HAWTHORNE STRAINER

1 ounce Gosling's Black Seal Rum

1 ounce Gosling's Gold Rum

2 ounces pineapple juice

2 ounces freshly squeezed orange juice

1 teaspoon grenadine (store-bought or homemade, page 45)

1 dash Angostura bitters

1 orange slice, for garnish

1 pineapple cube, for garnish

1 maraschino cherry, for garnish

Shake all liquid ingredients well with ice, and strain into a chilled rocks glasses filled with ice. Garnish with an orange slice, a pineapple cube, and a cherry, and serve.

Between the Sheets CITRUSY

COCKTAIL GLASS | KNIFE, JIGGER, SHAKER, HAWTHORNE STRAINER

1 ounce white rum

1 ounce Cognac

1 ounce Cointreau

½ ounce freshly squeezed lemon juice

1 lemon twist (see page 49), for garnish

Shake all liquid ingredients well with cracked ice. Strain into a chilled cocktail glass, garnish with a twist of lemon, and serve.

Blue Hawaiian FRUITY

TALL GLASS | JIGGER, BLENDER

3 ounces pineapple juice
1 ounce sweet-and-sour mix
¾ ounce light rum
¾ ounce vodka
½ ounce blue Curaçao liqueur
1 cocktail umbrella, for garnish

In a blender, blend all ingredients with ice until smooth.
Pour into a chilled tall glass, garnish with a brightly colored
umbrella, and serve.

Bushwacker CREAMY

HURRICANE GLASS | JIGGER, BLENDER, ZESTER OR GRATER

½ ounce rum
½ ounce vodka
½ ounce Irish cream liqueur
½ ounce Kahlúa
½ ounce amaretto
½ ounce chocolate liqueur
½ ounce hazelnut liqueur, such as Frangelico (optional)
½ ounce crème de coconut
1 cup crushed ice
Whipped cream, for topping
1 maraschino cherry, for garnish
3 dashes freshly grated nutmeg, for garnish

In a blender, blend all the liquid ingredients with the ice. Pour
into a chilled hurricane glass, top with whipped cream, garnish with a cherry and grated nutmeg, and serve.

The Cable Car FRUITY

 Tony Abou-Ganim, Las Vegas

COCKTAIL GLASS | KNIFE, JIGGER, HAWTHORNE STRAINER

Sugar-cinnamon rim (see page 49)
1½ ounces Captain Morgan Original Spiced Rum
¾ ounce Marie Brizard Orange Curaçao
1 ounce freshly squeezed lemon juice
½ ounce Simple Syrup (page 44)
1 orange spiral (see page 49), for garnish

Shake all liquid ingredients with ice until well blended. Strain into a chilled sugar cinnamon–rimmed cocktail glass, garnish with the orange spiral, and serve.

Calle Ocho Old Fashioned STRONG, EARTHY

Julio Cabrera, Ball & Chain, Miami

ROCKS GLASS | JIGGER, MIXING GLASS, BAR SPOON, HAWTHORNE STRAINER

2 ounces Bacardi 8 aged rum
½ ounce Demerara Syrup (page 44)
3 dashes Tobacco bitters*
1 tobacco leaf, for garnish

In a mixing glass, stir all liquid ingredients with ice. Strain into a chilled rocks glass over fresh ice, garnish with the tobacco leaf, and serve.

Tobacco bitters: Soak 2 tablespoons fresh tobacco leaves in Angostura bitters for 1 to 2 hours. Strain and bottle.

Corn 'n' Oil TROPICAL
ROCKS GLASS | KNIFE, JIGGER, BAR SPOON

2 ounces blackstrap rum
½ ounce falernum*
½ ounce freshly squeezed lime juice
3 dashes Angostura bitters
1 lime wedge, for garnish

In a chilled rocks glass, stir all liquid ingredients with crushed ice. Garnish with the lime wedge, and serve.

*A Caribbean cocktail staple. Falernum is the name for both a syrup and a liqueur made with cloves, lime zest, and almond. Search out John D. Taylor's Velvet Falernum.

El Presidente STRONG, CITRUSY
COCKTAIL GLASS | KNIFE, JIGGER, MIXING GLASS, BAR SPOON, HAWTHORNE STRAINER

1½ ounces white rum
1½ ounces white vermouth
1 bar spoon orange Curaçao or Grand Marnier
½ bar spoon grenadine (store-bought or homemade, page 45)
1 thinly cut orange peel, for garnish
1 maraschino cherry, for garnish (optional)

In a mixing glass, stir all liquid ingredients well with cracked ice. Strain into a chilled cocktail glass. Twist a swatch of thinly cut orange peel over the top, and drop it in or discard. Garnish with the cherry (if using), and serve.

Floridita CITRUSY

COCKTAIL GLASS | KNIFE, JIGGER, SHAKER, HAWTHORNE STRAINER

2 ounces white rum
¾ ounce freshly squeezed lime juice
1 teaspoon Simple Syrup (page 44)
1 teaspoon maraschino cherry liqueur
1 thin lime slice, for garnish

Shake all liquid ingredients well with ice, and strain into a chilled cocktail glass. Garnish with the lime slice, and serve.

The Getaway CITRUSY, EARTHY

Derek Brown, Washington, D.C.

COCKTAIL GLASS | JIGGER, SHAKER, HAWTHORNE STRAINER

1 ounce Cruzan Black Strap Rum
1 ounce freshly squeezed lemon juice
½ ounce Cynar
½ ounce Simple Syrup (page 44)

Shake all ingredients well with ice. Strain into a chilled cocktail glass, and serve.

Gully Brood CITRUSY

Beckaly Franks, Hong Kong

COLLINS GLASS | KNIFE, JIGGER, SHAKER, HAWTHORNE STRAINER

¾ ounce mezcal
¾ ounce Campari liqueur
¾ ounce Rabarbaro Zucca
½ ounce freshly squeezed lime juice
½ ounce Rich Simple Syrup (page 44)
1 grapefruit twist (see page 49), for garnish

Shake all liquid ingredients well with ice, and strain into a chilled Collins glass full of crushed ice. Garnish with a grapefruit twist, and serve.

Honi Makai CITRUSY
Hadi Ktiri, French 75, New Orleans

ROCKS GLASS | KNIFE, JIGGER, SHAKER, HAWTHORNE STRAINER

1½ ounces aged rum
¾ ounce lime juice
½ ounce overproof rum
½ ounce orange juice
¼ ounce allspice dram
¼ ounce orgeat (store-bought or homemade, page 46)
¼ ounce Herbsaint
1 fresh mint sprig, for garnish
1 pineapple leaf, for garnish
1 orange wheel (see page 49), for garnish

Shake all liquid ingredients well with ice. Strain into a chilled rocks glass, garnish with a mint sprig, pineapple leaf, and orange wheel, and serve.

Jungle Bird CITRUSY, FRUITY
ROCKS GLASS | JIGGER, SHAKER, HAWTHORNE STRAINER

1½ ounces blackstrap rum
1½ ounces pineapple juice
¾ ounces Campari liqueur
½ ounces freshly squeezed lime juice
½ ounces Simple Syrup (page 44)

Shake all ingredients well with ice, strain into a chilled rocks glass filled with crushed ice, and serve.

Knickerbocker FRUITY
DOUBLE OLD FASHIONED GLASS | JIGGER, SHAKER

2½ ounces golden rum
1½ teaspoons raspberry syrup
½ teaspoon orange Curaçao
½ ounce freshly squeezed lime juice, reserving half the spent shell
Berries, for garnish

Shake all liquid ingredients well with ice. Place the spent
shell of half a lime in a double old fashioned glass. Pour the
drink and ice into the glass, garnish with seasonal berries,
and serve.

Mai Tai TROPICAL, CITRUSY
COLLINS GLASS OR TIKI MUG | JIGGER, SHAKER

2 ounces dark rum
1 ounce freshly squeezed lime juice, reserving half the spent shell
½ ounce orange Curaçao
½ ounce orgeat (store-bought or homemade, page 46)
⅛ ounce Simple Syrup (page 44)
1 fresh mint sprig, for garnish

Shake all liquid ingredients well with ice, and pour unstrained
into a large chilled Collins glass. If making two or more, you
might want to strain the mixture into the glasses, and then
pour in the ice to ensure even pours. Garnish with half a lime
shell and a sprig of mint and serve.

RUM

Mary Pickford FRUITY

COCKTAIL GLASS | JIGGER, SHAKER, HAWTHORNE STRAINER

2 ounces white rum
1 ounce pineapple juice
1 bar spoon grenadine (store-bought or homemade, page 45)
1 bar spoon maraschino cherry liqueur
1 brandied cherry, for garnish

Shake all liquid ingredients well with ice. Strain into a chilled cocktail glass, garnish with the cherry, and serve.

Navy Grog STRONG

DOUBLE OLD FASHIONED GLASS | JIGGER, ICE CONE MOLD, SHAKER, HAWTHORNE STRAINER

1 ounce gold rum
1 ounce dark Jamaica rum
1 ounce white rum
1 ounce Honey Syrup (page 44)
¾ ounce freshly squeezed lime juice
¾ ounce white grapefruit juice
¾ ounce club soda
Ice cone*

Shake all liquid ingredients with ice, strain into a chilled double old fashioned glass containing your ice cone, and serve.

Ice cone kits are available online. Ice cones are made by packing shaved ice around a metal straw and then refreezing the cone until it is solid.

THE CLASSIC & CRAFT COCKTAIL RECIPE BOOK

Piña Colada TROPICAL, CREAMY
TALL GLASS | JIGGER, BLENDER

3 ounces pineapple juice
2½ ounces golden rum
1 ounce coconut cream
1 cup ice
Fruit, for garnish

In a blender, blend to combine the liquid ingredients. Add in a cube or two of ice at a time until the entire cup is fully incorporated, and blend until smooth. Pour into a chilled tall glass, garnish with fruit, and serve.

Planter's Punch CITRUSY
COLLINS GLASS | JIGGER, MIXING GLASS, BAR SPOON, HAWTHORNE STRAINER

3 ounces dark rum
1 ounce freshly squeezed lime juice
½ ounce freshly squeezed lemon juice
½ ounce grenadine (store-bought or homemade, page 45)
1 teaspoon Simple Syrup (page 44)
Straw

In a mixing glass, stir all ingredients well with cracked ice. Strain into a chilled Collins glass full of cracked ice, garnish with a straw and whatever you have on hand, and serve.

Princess CITRUSY
COUPE GLASS | JIGGER, SHAKER, HAWTHORNE STRAINER

2 ounces white rum
¾ ounce freshly squeezed lemon juice
¾ ounce Honey Syrup (page 44)

Shake all ingredients with ice, strain into a chilled coupe glass, and serve.

Queen's Park Swizzle CITRUSY, TROPICAL
COLLINS GLASS | JIGGER, BAR SPOON, MUDDLER

8 to 10 fresh mint leaves
3 ounces 80 proof demerara rum
½ ounce Rich Simple Syrup (page 44)
½ ounce freshly squeezed lime juice
2 dashes Angostura bitters
1 fresh mint sprig, for garnish

In a chilled Collins glass, gently bruise the mint leaves, using a muddler to move the leaves along the sides of the glass to coat it with mint. Add all liquid ingredients, and fill the glass with crushed ice. Use a bar spoon to swizzle the drink by gently twirling it between the palms of your hands until frost forms on the glass. Top with additional ice, garnish with the mint sprig, and serve.

THE CLASSIC & CRAFT COCKTAIL RECIPE BOOK

Rum Runner TROPICAL, FRUITY
HURRICANE GLASS | KNIFE, JIGGER, BLENDER, BAR SPOON

1 ounce light rum
1 ounce dark rum or aged rum
1 ounce pineapple juice
1 ounce freshly squeezed orange juice
1 ounce blackberry liqueur
1 ounce banana liqueur
Splash grenadine (store-bought or homemade, page 45)
½ ounce 151 proof rum, to float (see page 57)
1 slice pineapple, for garnish
Straw

In a blender, blend all liquid ingredients except the 151 proof
rum until smooth. Pour into a chilled hurricane glass. Float the
151 proof rum on top, garnish with a slice of pineapple and a
straw, and serve.

Test Pilot TROPICAL, CITRUSY
DOUBLE OLD FASHIONED GLASS | JIGGER, BLENDER

1½ ounces dark Jamaica rum
¾ ounce light rum
½ ounce freshly squeezed lime juice
½ ounce falernum
3 teaspoons Cointreau
⅛ teaspoon Pernod (or absinthe)
1 dash Angostura bitters
Skewer with 1 maraschino cherry, for garnish

In a blender, blend all liquid ingredients with 1 cup crushed
ice for 5 seconds, and then pour into a chilled double old
fashioned glass. Add more crushed ice to fill the glass, garnish
with a skewered cherry, and serve.

Zombie FRUITY

COLLINS GLASS | JIGGER, MIXING GLASS, BAR SPOON

1½ ounces golden rum
1 ounce dark rum
1 ounce freshly squeezed lime juice
½ ounce white rum
¼ ounce Simple Syrup (page 44)
1 teaspoon pineapple juice
1 teaspoon papaya juice
½ ounce 151 proof rum, to float (see page 57)
Straw
1 fresh mint sprig and/or fruit, for garnish (optional)

In a mixing glass, stir all liquid ingredients except the
151 proof rum well with ice, and pour into a chilled Collins
glass three-quarters full of crushed ice. Float the 151 on top.
If you wish, set the 151 on fire. Garnish with a straw and a mint
sprig or fruit, if desired, and serve.

CHAPTER EIGHT

MEZCAL & TEQUILA

In recent years, tequila and mezcal have become infinitely more refined and sippable. Despite the strides in production, the two spirits are still surrounded by some mystique and a lot of misinformation. Both spirits are distilled from agave, a flowering plant that grows all over Mexico that must be tended for several years before it can be fermented and distilled.

BEFORE THE SPANISH BROUGHT DISTILLATION to Mexico in the 1600s, a fermented drink made from agave known as *pulque* was drunk socially and in Aztec religious ceremonies. It is likely that the Spanish exploited this drink as an easy source of fermented sugars for their stills.

Although they are both made from agave, there are many differences between mezcal and tequila. First, tequila is a type of mezcal, just as bourbon is a type of whiskey. While mezcal can be made from any variety of agave, tequila must be made only from blue agave. Tequila is produced in five states in Mexico, but the majority is made in the state of Jalisco, while mezcal is made in smaller areas scattered around several states. In these regions, agave plants are grown for several years before they are harvested, and the sharp outer leaves are removed. The heart of the plant, called the *piña*, is then steamed or cooked at a low temperature to release the juice. Though the pulp is usually used as animal feed or fuel, some tequila makers add a bit of it to the tequila fermentation tanks to strengthen the agave flavor.

When you are buying tequila, keep an eye out for "100 percent de agave" on the label. Tequila makers can mix agave juice with sugar as long as it is made from at least 51 percent agave and labeled as a *mixto*. This mixture is then fermented, distilled, and bottled. Though some mixtos are made with the same care and attention as those made from 100 percent agave, many are not.

Unofficially, tequila is made in two broad styles that subtly impact how it will taste: highland and Tequila Valley. Just like climate affects whiskey aging, it also affects how flavors in the agave develop during its time in the ground. Generally, Tequila Valley tequilas tend to have darker flavors, like baking spice and slight pepper, while the more varied climate in the highlands can result in citrusy, delicate flavors.

Using tequila in respectable cocktails is a newer trend than even using vodka. The Margarita (page 174), arguably the most famous tequila cocktail, first appeared in the 1940s, but it did not become truly popular until the '70s. However, its history is murky at best and a complete unknown at worst. With that said, high-quality mezcal and tequila are pretty much ubiquitous now at craft cocktail bars for both sipping and mixing—and that is a wonderful thing.

Types of Mezcal and Tequila

Tequila is tequila and mezcal is mezcal, right? Fortunately for us, it is a bit more complicated. Traditionally, unaged tequilas have been the most common, but other, higher-dollar and higher-quality products have come on the market. These spirits range from unaged, vegetal potions to more expensive barrel-aged beauties.

Mezcal: Mezcal is one of the most misunderstood spirits. Like tequila, it is made from agave, but it can be made from any variety, and it can be made in several Mexican states. But after the harvest, the agaves used in mezcal are slowly roasted using the method native to the region. Typically, the roasting process imbues the final product with a smokiness comparable to Scotch. Mezcal can be sipped neat, but it can also be substituted for tequila in almost any cocktail for a smokier concoction. For starters, never, ever buy a bottle containing a worm: The inclusion is not a sign of quality but a cheap tourist attraction.

Tequila blanco (or plata): *Blanco* (white) tequilas, also called *plata* (silver), are not aged in barrels but can rest in a container for up to 60 days. Though some are slightly rougher than their barrel-aged counterparts, they tend to have a full, rich agave flavor. For this reason, many aficionados prefer to sip young tequila. This varietal is the most versatile in cocktails and infusions. It is available as a mixto and 100 percent agave.

Oro: Many oro tequilas are artificially colored mixtos. Others begin as unaged blanco that is blended with a small quantity of older tequila to add richness and depth. Typically, cheap gold tequilas tend to be in the well at most bars for their price, but 100 percent agave varietals are also available.

Reposado: A *reposado* or "rested" tequila is aged for 2 to 12 months in oak barrels. These tend to have less burn than blancos and are less complex than añejos. These tend to be the briniest tequilas, and the stars of this category are the best for shooting. They also make delicious cocktails.

Añejo: Darker than reposado, añejo, or "aged," tequila tends to be more complex than less aged tequilas. These spend between 1 and 3 years in oak barrels and pick up more of the barrel's oaky character. Like well-aged whiskies, these tequilas tend to be more suited for sipping than mixing. But as with whiskies, if you are feeling adventurous or generous, mixing añejo tequilas in cocktails will not send you amiss. Try substituting for bourbon or rye whiskey in a stirred drink, or use to add depth to a tequila cocktail. You win either way.

Extra añejo: As tequila has become more of a premium spirit, the laws have changed. The newest category of tequila, extra añejo, has aged for longer than 3 years in oak barrels. Though 3 years is not long for whiskies and rums, leaving tequila in oak removes much of its agave character. Extra añejos are not usually stocked at bars. However, some tequila producers have been releasing older liquors for longer than you might guess.

Similar Spirits

Other than tequila, pulque is probably the most common agave-based alcoholic drink. Several others, including bacanora, raicilla, and sikul, are produced but are not yet commonly available in the United States.

Pulque: Traditionally, pulque is made from fermented agave. It is not a liquor, but it predates mezcal and tequila by more than a millennium. It tends to be low in alcohol content and rarely goes above 8 percent ABV. In Mexico, it is served two ways: *pulque curado*, which is mixed with fruit or oatmeal or other flavors, and pure pulque, which is the straight stuff. Usually, it is milky white and frothy, and it tends to be rather sour and viscous in either form.

Mezcal and Tequila Tips

The right style of tequila for mixing or sipping depends a lot on your personal preferences. Though mixtos have traditionally been painted as the bad guys, some producers make these with all the care that would go into making a 100 percent agave. But the quality will cost you. For most cocktails, a silver or gold tequila will be more than adequate. For a more luxe experience, use your favorite reposado instead. But for smoke, use a mezcal.

When sipping one of the higher-end tequilas or mezcals, break out a tall, slender 2-ounce glass or tasting glass rather than a tumbler. These spirits are often as complex and earthy as other barrel-aged libations and often a bit more vegetal, which makes them an easy go-to for whiskey lovers and newcomers alike.

Agave spirits' popularity have come with a darker side. The ecological effects of growing only one crop are not to be discounted, but tequila's popularity has also been accompanied by a decline in production standards to meet demand. Though agave-based spirits should definitely still be drunk, bartenders from across the United States have banded together to form a group that advocates for sustainable production. It is definitely worth checking out, and it is on the web at TequilaInterchangeProject.org.

CLASSIC
MEZCAL & TEQUILA
COCKTAILS

El Diablo FRUITY, TART
HIGHBALL GLASS | KNIFE, JIGGER, SHAKER, FINE STRAINER

1½ ounces reposado tequila
½ ounce crème de cassis
½ ounce freshly squeezed lime juice
2 to 3 ounces ginger beer
1 lime wedge, for garnish (optional)
1 fresh blackberry, for garnish (optional)

Shake all liquid ingredients except the ginger beer well with ice, and strain into a chilled Collins glass full of ice. Top with the ginger beer, garnish with the lime wedge and blackberry (if using), and serve.

Ginger el Diablo: *Substitute Ginger Tequila for tequila (page 36).*

Margarita CITRUSY
ROCKS GLASS | JIGGER, SHAKER, HAWTHORNE STRAINER

Coarse salt rim (see page 49)
2 ounces silver tequila
1 ounce Cointreau
1 ounce freshly squeezed lime juice

Shake all ingredients with cracked ice, strain into a chilled rocks glass with a coarse salt rim over ice, and serve.

Flavored Margarita: *Substitute ½ ounce flavored liqueur for ½ ounce Cointreau.*
Jalapeño Margarita: *Use Jalapeño Tequila (page 35).*
Grapefruit Margarita: *Add ½ ounce grapefruit juice.*
Watermelon Margarita: *Use Watermelon Tequila (page 36).*

Paloma TART
COLLINS GLASS | JIGGER, BAR SPOON

2 ounces tequila
¾ ounce freshly squeezed lime juice
Pinch salt
Grapefruit soda (Jarritos is best), for topping

In a Collins glass, combine all ingredients except the grapefruit soda. Add ice, top with the grapefruit soda, stir gently, and serve.

Pomegranate Paloma: *Substitute ½ ounce pomegranate juice for ½ ounce lime juice.*
Strawberry Paloma: *Substitute Strawberry Tequila (page 35) for tequila.*

Sangrita CITRUSY, SPICY
SHOT GLASS | JIGGER, MIXING GLASS, BAR SPOON

1 ounce freshly squeezed orange juice
¾ to 1 ounce freshly squeezed lime juice, to taste
½ ounce grenadine (store-bought or homemade, page 45)
3 dashes hot sauce or ¼ teaspoon chili powder

In a mixing glass, stir all ingredients, chill the mixing glass in the refrigerator, and serve as a chaser for a tequila shot.

Tequila Daisy CITRUSY

COCKTAIL GLASS | JIGGER, SHAKER, HAWTHORNE STRAINER

2 ounces Partida Reposado Tequila
½ ounce freshly squeezed lemon juice
½ ounce Simple Syrup (page 44)
½ ounce Grand Marnier
Splash club soda, for topping

Shake all ingredients except the club soda well with ice. Strain into a chilled cocktail glass, top with a small splash of club soda, and serve.

Brandy Daisy: *Substitute brandy for tequila.*
Gin Daisy: *Substitute gin for tequila.*
Rum Daisy: *Substitute rum for tequila.*
Whiskey Daisy: *Substitute whiskey for tequila.*

Tequila Sunrise FRUITY

HIGHBALL GLASS | KNIFE, JIGGER, BAR SPOON

1½ ounces tequila
4 ounces freshly squeezed orange juice
1 dash grenadine (store-bought or homemade, page 45),
  to float (see page 57)
1 orange slice, for garnish
1 maraschino cherry, for garnish

Pour the tequila and then the orange juice into a chilled highball glass. Float the grenadine on top, garnish with an orange slice and a cherry, and serve.

THE CLASSIC & CRAFT COCKTAIL RECIPE BOOK

CRAFT
MEZCAL & TEQUILA
COCKTAILS

The 212 TART

Aisha Sharpe & Willy Shine, New York City

COLLINS GLASS | KNIFE, JIGGER, SHAKER, HAWTHORNE STRAINER

2 ounces tequila
2 ounces ruby red grapefruit juice
1 ounce Aperol
1 orange twist (see page 49), for garnish

Shake all ingredients well with ice, and strain into a chilled Collins glass over ice. Garnish with an orange twist, and serve.

Acapulco TROPICAL, FRUITY

HIGHBALL GLASS | JIGGER, SHAKER, HAWTHORNE STRAINER

3 ounces pineapple juice
2 ounces grapefruit juice
1 ounce tequila
1 ounce gold rum

Shake all ingredients well with ice. Strain into a chilled highball glass full of ice, and serve.

Black Diamond STRONG, CITRUSY
ROCKS GLASS | JIGGER, SHAKER, HAWTHORNE STRAINER

Black salt rim (see page 49)
2 ounces Maestro Dobel Tequila
½ ounce agave nectar
½ ounce freshly squeezed lime juice

Shake all ingredients well with ice, strain into a chilled rocks glass with a black salt rim full of ice, and serve.

Black Sombrero COFFEE, STRONG
COCKTAIL GLASS | JIGGER, SHAKER

2 ounces Kahlúa
1 ounce tequila
1 ounce vodka

Shake all ingredients well with ice. Pour into a chilled cocktail glass, and serve.

The Brave SMOKY, CITRUSY
Anvil Bar & Refuge, Houston

RED WINE GLASS | KNIFE, JIGGER

1 ounce Del Maguey Chichicapa Mezcal
1 ounce Tequila Cabeza Blanco
½ ounce Averna
1 bar spoon Royal Combier
3 small mists Angostura bitters
Flamed orange peel (see page 48), for garnish

THE CLASSIC & CRAFT COCKTAIL RECIPE BOOK

In a chilled red wine glass, combine the first 4 ingredients. Swirl until mixed. Lightly coat the inside of the glass by misting in the bitters, but do not swirl again. Garnish with the flamed orange peel, and serve.

Chapala STRONG, CITRUSY
ROCKS GLASS | KNIFE, JIGGER, SHAKER, HAWTHORNE STRAINER

1½ ounces tequila
2 teaspoons grenadine (store-bought or homemade, page 45)
¼ ounce freshly squeezed orange juice
¼ ounce freshly squeezed lemon juice
1 dash Triple Sec
Orange slice, for garnish

Shake all ingredients well with ice, and strain into a chilled rocks glass filled with ice. Garnish with the orange slice, and serve.

Classic Tequila Shot STRONG
SHOT GLASS | KNIFE, JIGGER

1½ ounces tequila
1 lime wedge
Pinch salt

Pour the tequila into a shot glass. Rub the lime wedge on the back of your thumb. Pinch the salt onto your hand. Lick the salt, gulp down the tequila, and bite the lime wedge.

Death Flip CREAMY, HERBAL

Chris Hysted, Black Pearl, Melbourne, Australia

SOUR GLASS | JIGGER, SHAKER, HAWTHORNE STRAINER,
ZESTER OR GRATER

1 ounce blanco tequila
½ ounce yellow Chartreuse
½ ounce Jägermeister liqueur
1 dash Vanilla Simple Syrup (page 44)
1 whole egg
Freshly grated nutmeg, for garnish

Shake all ingredients except the nutmeg vigorously without ice. Add ice, and shake vigorously again. Strain into a chilled sour glass, garnish with the freshly grated nutmeg, and serve.

Del Rio STRONG, BITTER

Scott Baird, Bon Vivants, San Francisco

COUPE GLASS | KNIFE, JIGGER, MIXING GLASS, BAR SPOON,
HAWTHORNE STRAINER

1½ ounces Tequila Ocho Plata
¾ ounce manzanilla sherry
¾ ounce elderflower liqueur, preferably St-Germain
2 to 3 dashes Angostura orange bitters
1 grapefruit twist (see page 49), for garnish

In a mixing glass, stir all liquid ingredients well with ice. Strain into a chilled coupe glass, garnish with the grapefruit twist, and serve.

El Compadre STRONG, FRUITY
COCKTAIL GLASS | JIGGER, SHAKER

1½ ounces tequila
½ teaspoon maraschino cherry liqueur
1 teaspoon grenadine (store-bought or homemade, page 45)
2 dashes orange bitters (store-bought or homemade, page 40)

Shake all ingredients with ice, strain into a chilled cocktail glass, and serve.

El Peppino Fresco FRESH, HERBAL
Shane Tison, The Randolph at Broome, New York City

DOUBLE ROCKS GLASS | KNIFE, JIGGER, SHAKER, MUDDLER

2 cucumber slices, plus 1 more for garnish
2 ounces tequila
1 ounce freshly squeezed lime juice
½ ounce elderflower liqueur, preferably St-Germain
½ ounce Simple Syrup (page 44)
1 dash Peychaud's bitters

In a shaker, muddle 2 cucumber slices and add the next 4 ingredients. Shake with ice, and pour into a chilled double rocks glass. Finish with a dash of Peychaud's bitters, garnish with a slice of cucumber, and serve.

Frostbite CREAMY, SWEET

ROCKS GLASS | JIGGER, SHAKER, HAWTHORNE STRAINER

1½ ounces tequila
½ ounce white crème de cacao
½ ounce blue Curaçao
½ ounce cream
1 maraschino cherry, for garnish

Shake the liquid ingredients well with ice, and strain into a chilled rocks glass full of ice. Garnish with a maraschino cherry, and serve.

Into the Void STRONG, HERBAL

Bobby Eldridge, The Broken Shaker, Miami

ROCKS GLASS | KNIFE, JIGGER, MIXING GLASS, BAR SPOON, HAWTHORNE STRAINER

1 ounce Cocchi Rosa
¾ ounce Bruto Americano
½ ounce Ilegal Mezcal Joven
½ ounce Altos Reposado tequila
6 dashes Luxardo maraschino liqueur
1 orange peel, for garnish

In a mixing glass, stir all liquid ingredients well with ice. Strain into a chilled rocks glass over 1 large ice cube, garnish with the orange peel, and serve.

Jaguar HERBAL, PEPPERY

Tom Schlesinger-Guidelli, Eastern Standard, Boston

COCKTAIL GLASS | KNIFE, JIGGER, MIXING GLASS, BAR SPOON,
HAWTHORNE STRAINER

1½ ounces blanco tequila
¾ ounce Amer Picon
½ ounce green Chartreuse
3 dashes Fee Brothers West Indian Orange Bitters
1 flamed orange peel (see page 48), for garnish

In a mixing glass, stir all liquid ingredients well with ice.
Strain into a chilled cocktail glass, flame an orange twist over
the drink, and serve.

Matador FRUITY

ROCKS GLASS | JIGGER, SHAKER, HAWTHORNE STRAINER

3 ounces pineapple juice
1½ ounces gold tequila
½ ounce freshly squeezed lime juice

Shake all ingredients well with ice. Strain into a chilled rocks
glass full of ice and serve.

Matador (frozen) FRUITY

COLLINS GLASS | KNIFE, JIGGER, BLENDER

½ cup crushed ice
2 ounces tequila
¼ cup pineapple chunks
½ ounce Simple Syrup (page 44) or Triple Sec
½ ounce freshly squeezed lime juice

In a blender, blend all ingredients until smooth. Pour into a chilled Collins glass, and serve.

Mexican Madras FRUITY, TART
ROCKS GLASS | KNIFE, JIGGER, SHAKER, HAWTHORNE GLASS

3 ounces cranberry juice
1 ounce gold tequila
½ ounce freshly squeezed orange juice
1 dash freshly squeezed lime juice
1 orange slice, for garnish

Shake all liquid ingredients well with ice, and strain into a chilled rocks glass. Garnish with an orange slice, and serve.

Shady Lady FRUITY
HIGHBALL GLASS | KNIFE, JIGGER

4 ounces white grapefruit juice
1 ounce white tequila
1 ounce Midori
1 lime wedge, for garnish
1 maraschino cherry, for garnish

Pour all liquid ingredients into a chilled highball glass full of ice. Garnish with a lime and a cherry, and serve.

Tequila Cocktail STRONG, CITRUSY

COCKTAIL GLASS | JIGGER, SHAKER, HAWTHORNE STRAINER

2 ounces tequila
1 ounce freshly squeezed lime juice
½ ounce grenadine (store-bought or homemade, page 45)
Dash orange flower water

Shake all ingredients with ice. Strain into a chilled cocktail glass, and serve.

Tijuana Speedball CREAMY

Felicia Sledge, Saucebox, Portland, Oregon

COCKTAIL GLASS | JIGGER, SHAKER, HAWTHORNE STRAINER

1½ ounces cold espresso
1 ounce reposado tequila
½ ounce Kahlúa
½ ounce Irish cream liqueur, such as Baileys Irish Cream
Pinch ground cinnamon, for topping

Shake all liquid ingredients well, and strain into a chilled cocktail glass. Sprinkle cinnamon on top, and serve.

CHAPTER NINE
VODKA

In the cocktail world, vodka occupies a very strange space. Some craft cocktail bars refuse to carry it, and some bartenders will rail against its neutrality. Others hail its versatility as an easy way to get new customers to try craft cocktails without taking them too far outside their comfort zone. Within the bar industry, the common refrain is that "vodka pays the bills," and for many, it does. Unlike other spirits, differences between brands often come down to minute differences in texture and extremely subtle differences in taste and aroma.

BUT WHAT, EXACTLY, IS VODKA? Legally, it is a distilled spirit made from any fermentable ingredient. It is basically an unaged, higher-proof version of all other liquors in existence. Vodka has been distilled from everything from milk and rice to wheat and grapes. Despite its reputation for being a potato-based Russian spirit, only about 5 percent is actually produced using spuds.

Several countries claim to be the birthplace of vodka, most notably Poland and Russia. Any way you cut, the spirit has been around for more than a millennium. Surprisingly enough, vodka was not made in the United States until 1934. It started gaining steam in the late '40s, and by the '60s it was outselling gin, in no small measure thanks to some truly creative advertising campaigns.

More than a few of these targeted women, and one led to the enduring myth that vodka is a lower-calorie alternative to other booze. While some vodkas are, several gins and whiskies clock in with fewer calories. To make matters more complex, dietitians disagree over whether alcohol calories affect the body the same way as food calories. Regardless of the health benefits, we will take the excuse to drink it. To vodka!

Types of Vodka

Dividing vodka into categories is a difficult and arguably pointless task. If categorized by country, the list becomes a recitation of brands and their attributes rather than a discussion of their stylistic differences. Though some brands within countries may have some similarities, these traits are not necessarily indicative of a nationwide trend. The same is true for separation by the base ingredient. Since vodka can be distilled from anything, categorizing them this way also threatens to become a list of brands. Instead, it may be more effective to look at the terms and definitions that are used in labeling.

Number of distillations: All liquor is distilled at least once, much of it twice. Usually, it is made with stills that contain an extra processing chamber to remove any traces of compounds that add flavor to other spirits. With vodka, the label often includes the number of distillations that the spirit has undergone. Though it sounds cool, there is not a regulated definition of "distilled," so this trait arguably impacts the final product less than, say, the raw ingredients or the water used in its production. Further, many vodka brands opt to buy their distillate and redistill it to claim it as their own. This practice also bumps up the number of distillations, making it difficult to suss out whether a product was actually crafted at a given site.

Raw ingredients: Many brands tout their raw ingredients as a differentiator. This labeling is closer to the mark: A rye-based vodka will have more vanilla and pepper flavor, while a wheat vodka will be softer and more delicate. Well-done potato vodkas can be rich and creamy, while vodka made from corn is often slightly sweet. One note: Vodka distilled from wheat is probably not necessarily going to be okay for gluten-intolerant folks to drink. Experts differ on whether the distillation process strips out the gluten. With that said, vodka produced from other ingredients should be all right. Examine flavored vodkas on a case-by-case basis.

Filtration: After distillation, vodka is filtered. Most producers use activated charcoal to remove harshness and unwanted flavors, but others have experimented with other means of filtration, such as sand and, in one case, ground diamonds. More expensive vodkas are pumped through columns of charcoal, while cheaper ones may be steeped with it.

Some home drinkers have used the same idea to improve the flavor of vodka they have on hand. Though you can boost the quality of your hooch by running it through an activated charcoal water filter, these filters are expensive. Ultimately, it may be more cost-effective to spring for the better-quality vodka up front.

Flavorings: It may seem like a modern trend, but adding flavor to neutral hooch has been done for centuries. With that said, those products would have likely been much rougher than their modern equivalents. Herbs and spices would have been added to mask

VODKA

unpleasant flavors, or sometimes to preserve the delicate, seasonal ingredients. Nowadays, the goal is to boost sales rather than to preserve anything. Even premium brands produce flavored vodkas, usually using natural ingredients. Many more are made with artificial flavorings and sweeteners. The flavors you will find on shelves range from the usual grapefruit, orange, and vanilla to more eccentric and sometimes off-putting flavors like Cinnabon cinnamon roll, bacon, electricity, and grass.

Similar Spirits

These liquors may resemble vodka, but they are not actually subtypes of the spirit.

Aguardiente: With a name that translates from Portuguese as "burned water," aguardiente is similar to cachaça (page 148) but can be made from just about any ingredient. It is made differently in each country but is often made from grapes.

Shochu: Japan's national spirit can be made from any raw ingredient but tends to be distilled to a much lower proof than vodka. More than half is distilled from barley, but it is also produced from sweet potatoes, rice, and buckwheat. The different styles of shochu are more varied than vodka: Some is aged in wood, some is distilled multiple times, and some is fermented with mold rather than yeast. It contains no sugar, but many styles are not available outside Japan.

Vodka Tips

Outside of the United States, vodka is not usually mixed into cocktails outside of the occasional vodka martini. In many Northern and Eastern European countries, vodka is drunk chilled with food. Storing it in the freezer helps achieve the thicker, richer texture, also called viscosity, that is an extremely desirable trait in vodka. Usually, it is served neat in a small glass and is to be sipped, not shot. Though some drink it with ice rather than neat, others will pooh-pooh the practice because it dilutes the vodka.

To best enjoy vodka, make sure that the glassware you will use is spotlessly clean. Avoid strongly scented dish detergents to clean this glassware, as the scent can interfere with your overall experience. Many will suggest that only premium vodkas be drunk this way, but as mentioned, defining what makes a premium or ultra-premium vodka is extremely difficult.

If you are looking to experience vodka the European way, chill it down while you stock up on snacks like rustic-style rye bread, herring, caviar, dill pickles, ham, and borscht. Serve your feast with some mineral water, and alternate bites of food and sips of vodka.

For vodka cocktails, excluding the Vodka Martini (page 118), use a midrange vodka good enough to drink neat, but cheap enough to shoot without budgetary concerns. Many vodka cocktails are designed to mask the taste of alcohol, so its quality is less of a concern than if you are drinking it neat.

CLASSIC
VODKA COCKTAILS

Black Russian COFFEE
ROCKS GLASS | JIGGER, BAR SPOON

2 ounces vodka
1 ounce Kahlúa

Pour both ingredients into a chilled rocks glass filled with ice.
Stir gently, and serve.

White Russian: *Add 1 ounce heavy cream.*
Brave Bull: *Substitute tequila for vodka.*
Dirty Mother: *Substitute brandy for vodka.*
Russian Bear: *Substitute crème de cacao for Kahlúa and add
1 ounce heavy cream.*

Bloody Mary SAVORY, TOMATOEY
COLLINS GLASS | JIGGER, SHAKER, HAWTHORNE STRAINER

4 ounces tomato juice
2 ounces vodka
½ tablespoon freshly squeezed lemon juice
1 teaspoon horseradish
1 splash Worcestershire sauce
3 dashes hot sauce, preferably Tabasco
Pinch salt
Freshly ground black pepper
1 celery stalk, for garnish (optional)

Shake all liquid ingredients well with cracked ice, and strain into a chilled Collins glass with 2 or 3 ice cubes in it. Add a pinch of salt and a bit of freshly ground pepper, to taste. Garnish with the stalk of celery (if using) and serve.

Bloody Maria: *Substitute tequila for vodka.*
Red Snapper: *Substitute gin for vodka.*

Cosmopolitan FRUITY, TART

Adapted from Toby Cecchini's recipe

MARTINI GLASS | KNIFE, JIGGER, SHAKER, HAWTHORNE STRAINER

2 ounces citron vodka
1 ounce cranberry juice
1 ounce freshly squeezed lime juice
1 ounce Triple Sec
1 orange peel, for garnish

Shake all liquid ingredients well with ice, and strain into a chilled martini glass. Garnish with an orange peel, and serve.

Rude Cosmopolitan: *Substitute tequila for vodka.*
Ginger Cosmopolitan: *Muddle 3 or 4 slices of ginger before adding ingredients.*
Metropolitan: *Substitute currant-flavored vodka for citron vodka.*
Crantini: *Omit Triple Sec and lime juice, and substitute Cranberry Vodka (page 37). Garnish with fresh cranberries.*

Greyhound TART
ROCKS GLASS | JIGGER, BAR SPOON

4 ounces grapefruit juice
2 ounces vodka

In a chilled rocks glass half full of ice, stir both ingredients gently to combine, and serve.

Salty Dog: *Rim glass with salt (see page 49).*
Salty Chihuahua: *Rim glass with salt (see page 49), and substitute tequila for vodka.*

Moscow Mule TART, SPICY
MOSCOW MULE MUG OR COLLINS GLASS | KNIFE, JIGGER

½ lime
2 ounces vodka
4 to 6 ounces ginger beer
Stirring rod

Squeeze the lime half into a chilled Moscow Mule mug or Collins glass, and drop in the spent shell. Fill the glass halfway with ice, pour in the vodka, and top with cold ginger beer. Serve with a stirring rod.

Mexican Mule: *Substitute tequila for vodka.*
Kentucky Mule: *Substitute bourbon for vodka.*
Gin Gin Mule: *Substitute gin for vodka.*

Screwdriver CITRUSY
ROCKS GLASS | JIGGER, BAR SPOON

4 ounces freshly squeezed orange juice
2 ounces vodka

Pour both ingredients into a chilled rocks glass half full of ice, stir gently to combine, and serve.

Madras: *Cut orange juice to 1 ounce and add 4 ounces cranberry juice.*
Harvey Wallbanger: *Float ½ ounce Galliano on top (see page 57).*
Freddy Fudpucker: *Substitute tequila for vodka and float ½ ounce of Galliano on top (see page 57).*

CRAFT
VODKA COCKTAILS

Absolute Stress FRUITY
COLLINS GLASS | KNIFE, JIGGER, SHAKER, HAWTHORNE STRAINER

1 ounce vodka
1 ounce dark rum
1 ounce peach schnapps
1 ounce freshly squeezed orange juice
1 ounce cranberry juice
1 orange slice, for garnish
1 cherry, for garnish

Shake all liquid ingredients well with ice, and strain into a
chilled Collins glass over ice. Garnish with a slice of orange
and a cherry, and serve.

Appletini TART, FRUITY
COCKTAIL GLASS | KNIFE, JIGGER, SHAKER, HAWTHORNE STRAINER

2 ounces vodka
1½ ounces sour apple liqueur
1½ teaspoons freshly squeezed lemon juice
1 green apple slice, for garnish

Shake all liquid ingredients well with ice until chilled through.
Strain into a chilled cocktail glass, garnish with the green
apple slice, and serve.

THE CLASSIC & CRAFT COCKTAIL RECIPE BOOK

Autumn Pear FRUITY, FRESH

Stefan Lange, The Otesaga Resort, Cooperstown, New York

MARTINI GLASS | KNIFE, JIGGER, SHAKER, HAWTHORNE STRAINER

1½ ounces Skyy Bartlett Pear Vodka
1 ounce Cointreau
½ ounce freshly squeezed lime juice
2 dashes grenadine (store-bought or homemade, page 45)
1 lime wedge, for garnish

Shake all liquid ingredients with ice, and strain into a chilled martini glass. Garnish with the lime wedge, and serve.

Bay Breeze TART, FRUITY

HIGHBALL GLASS | KNIFE, JIGGER

2 ounces cranberry juice
2 ounces pineapple juice
1½ ounces vodka
1 lime wedge, for garnish

Pour all liquid ingredients into a chilled highball glass full of ice. Garnish with a lime wedge, and serve.

Buffalo Green FRESH, SPICY

Osvaldo Vazquez, The Cape, Cabo San Lucas, Mexico

COLLINS GLASS | KNIFE, JIGGER, BAR SPOON

2 ounces fresh cucumber juice
¼ ounce freshly squeezed lime juice
6 ounces ginger beer
1½ ounces vodka
1 cucumber slice, for garnish

In a chilled Collins glass, stir all liquid ingredients for about 10 seconds to combine. Garnish with a slice of cucumber, and serve.

Cape Codder TART, FRUITY
HIGHBALL GLASS | KNIFE, JIGGER, BAR SPOON

4 ounces cranberry juice
2 ounces vodka
½ ounce freshly squeezed lime juice
1 lime wedge, for garnish

Pour all liquid ingredients into a chilled highball glass filled with ice, and stir gently to combine. Garnish with the lime wedge, and serve.

Chocolate Martini CREAMY, SWEET
MARTINI GLASS | JIGGER, SHAKER, HAWTHORNE STRAINER

2½ ounces half-and-half
1½ ounces chocolate liqueur
1½ ounces crème de cacao
½ ounce vodka

Shake all ingredients well with ice, strain into a chilled cocktail glass, and serve.

THE CLASSIC & CRAFT COCKTAIL RECIPE BOOK

Electric Lemonade SWEET, FRUITY
COLLINS GLASS | KNIFE, JIGGER, BAR SPOON

2 ounces sweet and sour mix
1½ ounces vodka
½ ounce blue Curaçao
4 ounces lemon-lime soda, for topping
1 lemon wedge

Pour the first 3 ingredients into a chilled Collins glass filled
with ice. Stir gently to combine, and top with lemon-lime soda.
Squeeze the lemon wedge over the drink, drop it in, and serve.

Espresso Martini COFFEE
COCKTAIL GLASS | JIGGER, SHAKER, HAWTHORNE STRAINER

2 ounces vodka
1 ounce Kahlúa
1 ounce espresso
Simple Syrup (page 44), to taste

Shake all ingredients well with ice. Strain into a chilled
cocktail glass, and serve.

Gypsy Queen STRONG
COCKTAIL GLASS | KNIFE, JIGGER, MIXING GLASS, BAR SPOON,
HAWTHORNE STRAINER

2 ounces vodka
1 ounce Bénédictine
2 dashes Angostura bitters
1 thin-cut lemon peel, for garnish

In a mixing glass, stir the liquid ingredients well with ice. Strain into a chilled cocktail glass. Twist a swatch of thin-cut lemon peel over the top, discard the peel, and serve.

Hairy Navel FRUITY, SWEET
HIGHBALL GLASS | JIGGER

1 ounce vodka
1 ounce peach schnapps
Freshly squeezed orange juice, for topping

Pour the vodka and peach schnapps into a chilled highball glass filled with ice cubes. Top with orange juice, and serve.

John Daly SWEET
COLLINS GLASS | JIGGER

1½ ounces vodka
Sweet tea, to fill glass halfway
Lemonade, to top

Pour the vodka into a chilled Collins glass filled with ice. Fill the glass halfway with sweet tea, top with lemonade, and serve.

Kamikaze TART, CITRUSY
ROCKS GLASS | JIGGER, SHAKER, HAWTHORNE STRAINER

2 ounces vodka
1 ounce Triple Sec
1 ounce freshly squeezed lime juice

Shake all ingredients well with ice, strain into a chilled rocks glass filled with ice, and serve.

Lemon Drop TART, SWEET

MARTINI GLASS | KNIFE, JIGGER, SHAKER, HAWTHORNE STRAINER

Sugar rim (see page 49)
1½ ounces citrus vodka
¾ ounce freshly squeezed lemon juice
½ ounce Triple Sec
½ ounce Simple Syrup (page 44)
1 twist of lemon peel (see page 49), for garnish

Shake all liquid ingredients with ice, and strain into a chilled, sugar-rimmed martini glass. Garnish with a twist of lemon, and serve.

Long Island Iced Tea SWEET, TEA

2 COLLINS GLASSES | KNIFE, JIGGER, SHAKER

1 ounce vodka
1 ounce gin
1 ounce white rum
1 ounce white tequila
½ ounce Triple Sec
2 tablespoons freshly squeezed lemon juice
4 ounces cola-flavored soda, preferably Coca-Cola, more or less
  to taste, for topping
2 lemon wedges, for garnish

Shake all the liquid ingredients except the cola-flavored soda well with ice. Pour into 2 chilled Collins glasses, and top with the cola. Garnish with lemon wedges, and serve.

Lüft's Zima CITRUSY, BUBBLY

Kate Gerwin, Lüft Bar, Bismarck, North Dakota

COLLINS GLASS | JIGGER, SHAKER, HAWTHORNE STRAINER

1½ ounces vodka
1 ounce Bols Yogurt Liqueur
1 ounce water
1 ounce Simple Syrup (page 44)
½ ounce freshly squeezed lemon juice
¼ ounce freshly squeezed lime juice
1 ounce club soda, for topping
Straw

Shake all ingredients except the club soda well with ice. Strain
into a chilled Collins glass filled with ice. Top with club soda
and a straw, and serve.

Melon Ball FRUITY, SWEET

ROCKS GLASS | JIGGER, MELON BALLER

2 ounces Midori
1 ounce vodka
Freshly squeezed orange juice, for topping
1 freshly scooped melon ball, for garnish (optional)

Pour the Midori and vodka into a chilled rocks glass full of ice.
Top with orange juice, garnish with a melon ball (if using),
and serve.

Mudslide CREAMY, SWEET

ROCKS GLASS | JIGGER, SHAKER, HAWTHORNE STRAINER, KNIFE

2 ounces Irish cream liqueur
1 ounce Kahlúa
1 ounce vodka
Bar chocolate, for topping

Shake the liquid ingredients, and strain into a chilled rocks glass full of ice. Use a knife to shave chocolate flakes on top, and serve.

Frozen Mudslide: *Use 1 ounce Irish cream. Combine ingredients in a blender with 3 scoops vanilla ice cream and 1 cup of ice. Blend until smooth, and serve in a chilled rocks glass.*

Pink Lemonade SWEET, CITRUSY

COUPE GLASS | JIGGER, SHAKER, HAWTHORNE STRAINER

1½ ounces vodka
1 ounce freshly squeezed lemon juice
1 ounce Simple Syrup (page 44)
½ ounce Chambord

Shake all ingredients well with ice, strain into a chilled coupe glass, and serve.

Pomegranate Martini TART, CITRUSY
MARTINI GLASS | JIGGER, SHAKER, HAWTHORNE STRAINER

6 ounces pomegranate juice
2 ounces Absolut citrus-infused vodka
1 ounce Cointreau
¼ ounce freshly squeezed lemon juice
Splash club soda (optional)
Pomegranate seeds, for garnish

Shake all liquid ingredients well with ice, and strain into a chilled martini glass. Garnish with pomegranate seeds and serve.

Russian Cadillac FRUITY, CREAMY
COCKTAIL GLASS | JIGGER, SHAKER, HAWTHORNE STRAINER

1 ounce vodka
1 ounce heavy cream
¾ ounce Galliano
¼ ounce white crème de cacao

Shake all ingredients well with ice, strain into a chilled cocktail glass, and serve.

Sea Breeze FRUITY
HIGHBALL GLASS | KNIFE, JIGGER

2 ounces cranberry juice
2 ounces grapefruit juice
1½ ounces vodka
1 lime wedge, for garnish

Pour the liquid ingredients into a chilled highball glass full of ice. Garnish with a lime wedge, and serve.

THE CLASSIC & CRAFT COCKTAIL RECIPE BOOK

Sex on the Beach 1 FRUITY, SWEET

HIGHBALL GLASS | KNIFE, JIGGER

1½ ounces vodka
1½ ounces cranberry juice
1½ ounces freshly squeezed orange juice
¾ ounce peach schnapps
1 orange slice, for garnish

Pour the liquid ingredients into a chilled highball glass filled
with ice. Garnish with a slice of orange, and serve.

Sex on the Beach 2 TROPICAL, FRUITY, SWEET

COUPE GLASS | JIGGER, BAR SPOON

1 ounce vodka
4 ounces cranberry juice
½ ounce Midori
½ ounce Chambord
Pineapple juice, for topping

In a chilled coupe glass, pour the vodka over crushed ice. Add
the next 3 ingredients, and top with the pineapple juice. Stir
gently, and serve.

Teatini TART

COCKTAIL GLASS | KNIFE, JIGGER, SHAKER, HAWTHORNE STRAINER

Sugar Rim (see page 49)
1¾ ounces Black Tea Vodka (page 37)
1 ounce sweet iced tea
¼ ounce freshly squeezed lemon juice
1 lemon wedge, for garnish

Shake all liquid ingredients well with ice, and strain into a
chilled cocktail glass rimmed with sugar. Garnish with a lemon
wedge, and serve.

Vodka Espresso Cocktail COFFEE

Dick Bradsell, London

COCKTAIL GLASS | JIGGER, SHAKER, HAWTHORNE STRAINER

2 ounces vodka
1 ounce espresso
½ ounce coffee liqueur
¼ ounce Simple Syrup (page 44)
3 coffee beans, for garnish

Shake all liquid ingredients with ice until chilled and foamy.
Strain into a chilled cocktail glass, garnish with the coffee
beans, and serve.

CHAPTER TEN

WHISKEY

Fire water, water of life, juice—whatever you call it, whiskey (also spelled **whisky**) is an entrancing subject. The amber-colored liquor varies hugely depending on where it is made, ranging from smoky Scotches to rough, unaged American whiskey and everything in between.

THE ROOTS OF WHISKEY-MAKING span back to fourteenth-century Ireland, or so the story goes. Back then, whiskey would have looked quite different: It would not have been aged in a barrel and would probably have been a lot rougher than what is available today. Despite the changes, one thing has stayed similar: the name. Then called *uisce beatha* (sometimes with alternate spelling), *uisce* was pronounced "ish-kee."

If you have snooped around the liquor store, you have probably noticed that some whiskies are labeled *whiskey* and others are labeled *whisky*. The current convention is that Irish and American whiskey is spelled with the *e*, and that Scotch, Canadian, and Japanese whisky is spelled without. But some bourbons and Tennessee whiskies—including Maker's Mark and George Dickel—are spelled without the *e*. But do not refer to Scotch as *whiskey*. Scotsmen will tell you that that is quite rude.

Wherever it is made, this spirit inspires strong feelings. Whiskey has a rich history and has been the tipple of choice for many well-known historical figures. Prime Minister Winston Churchill, actress Ava Gardner, and author Mark Twain were known to drink whatever whiskey was at hand, whereas singer Frank Sinatra loved Jack Daniel's Tennessee Whiskey.

Despite the differences within the category, all whiskey is made from some type of cereal grain. The exact grain that can be used, how it must be distilled, what barrels can be used to age it, and how long it must stay in the barrel varies depending on its country of origin. Further, all these aspects impact the resulting whiskey's color, scent, and taste, making them essential in the quest to differentiate different types of whiskey.

Generally, producers in Scotland, Ireland, and Japan primarily use malted barley. Some other grain whiskies are also produced within the countries, though they must be labeled as such. Canadian and American producers tend to distill rye, corn, wheat, malted barley, or some combination of those. But it is how the whiskies are treated after they are aged that leads to some of the most confusing and often misused terms in the business: *straight*, *blended*, and *single malt*.

THE CLASSIC & CRAFT COCKTAIL RECIPE BOOK

Straight: Straight whiskey is a peculiar legal definition in United States whiskey-making. According to law, it must be made from a grain mixture, known as the mash bill, of at least 51 percent of one type of grain. It must be under 80 percent ABV when it comes off the still and be at less than 62½ percent ABV when it is barreled. Further, it must be aged for at least 2 years in new oak barrels, but if it is aged less than 4, it must be labeled with its exact age. Bourbon, Tennessee whiskey, and American rye can all be straight whiskey. However, despite the moniker, types of straight whiskey "may include mixtures of two or more straight [whiskies] provided that all of the whiskies are produced in the same state," according to law. Strange, indeed.

Blended: Blended whiskey often gets a bad rap as being lighter bodied or lower quality. Although there is no question that poor-quality blends exist, most whiskey that is made is blended, but not all of it has to be labeled as such. In fact, unless a whiskey is explicitly labeled as a *single barrel*, it has likely been combined with other whiskies at some point in its production. In Scotland and Ireland, blended whiskey is defined two different ways. The first is as a mixture of barrel-aged malt whiskey and whiskey made from other grains. The second is as a mixture of malt whiskey from two or more distilleries, which is usually referred to as blended malt.

Much of the confusion (and stigma) toward blended whiskey comes from United States law. In the United States, blended whiskey is defined as a mixture of different straight whiskies *or* a combination of a straight spirit with a neutral spirit. Since the beginning of whiskey-making in the United States, blending has not been a significant part of the culture as it has in most other countries. It's likely that the bottom-shelf blends we are familiar with have colored our perception of what makes a blend.

Single malt: Despite the common misconception that single-malt whisky is made from a single barrel or batch, it is not. In Scotland and Ireland, single malt must be made from only malted barley at a single distillery. It may contain whiskey from many different barrels or batches or stills, as long as they were produced at the same distillery.

Types of Whiskey

Bourbon: Nicknamed "America's Native Spirit," bourbon is king in the United States. Though most other countries have a minimum age requirement, the United States does not (except for straight bourbons), a loophole that some producers take advantage of. It must be made from at least 51 percent corn, which gives it a softness and sweetness that pairs really well with citrus and vanilla.

Recently, bourbon's popularity has resulted in rising prices, both on the primary and resale markets. Some old standards are now difficult to find, and others have removed the age statement from their bottles, making suggestions for sipping bourbons more difficult. Generally, vanilla and caramel flavors peak somewhere between 9 and 15 or so years of aging, with oak gradually taking over beyond that point. But due to temperature fluctuations, warehouse quirks, and other factors, it is not a hard-and-fast rule.

For mixing, Four Roses Yellow Label, Old Grand-Dad 114, and Buffalo Trace are all solid liquor cabinet staples. If you can find it for a reasonable price, Elijah Craig Small Batch (formerly Elijah Craig 12 year) or Old Weller Antique 107 are great for either sipping or mixing. Above that price point, the value and quality vary wildly.

Tennessee whiskey: Though bourbon may be king within the United States, a Tennessee whiskey holds the title for world's best-selling whiskey (as of 2016). Legally, there are only a couple of minor variances between the two. For one, bourbon is defined at the federal level, while Tennessee whiskey is defined by both state and federal regulations. Although Tennessee whiskey must meet all the federal requirements for bourbon, it must be produced within the state's limits. Since 2014, it also must be "filtered through maple charcoal prior to aging," a step known as the Lincoln County Process.

This extra touch gives the whiskey a slightly smoky sweetness. Producers are capitalizing on it to make premium versions of their widely available product, and big names like Jack Daniel's and George Dickel have released limited-edition, single-barrel bottlings over the past few years.

Rye: Before bourbon was popular, Americans who drank whiskey drank rye. It provides a spicy backbone for cocktails, giving Manhattans and Whiskey Sours (pages 217 and 221, respectively) a fullness that many bourbons can not. In more recent years, its rough frontier reputation has mellowed, giving rise to a host of modern ryes that range from big and spicy to soft and round. The legal requirements are almost identical to those of bourbon, although rye whiskey must be made from 51 percent rye rather than corn.

As rye has become more popular, mainstream brands like Wild Turkey, Jack Daniel's, and Woodford Reserve have begun making their own. The range within these new products is incredible. For mixing, Rittenhouse Rye is still one of the best out there. For sipping, High West's Double Rye is quite pleasant. If you plan to splurge for a big anniversary, Willett has some pretty amazing sipping whiskies.

CANADIAN WHISKY

Out of all the whisky-producing countries in the world, Canada is probably the most misunderstood. Although many of the limited releases are amazing, it is not hard to see why it got a bad rap: In 2015, 75 percent of all Canadian whisky that was produced was shipped to the United States, but only about 10 percent of the premium products left Canada.

Legally, Canadian whisky regulations provide producers a lot of leeway for experimenting. Whisky must be distilled from grain to at least 40 percent ABV and aged in wood for no less than 3 years. Any whisky produced in Canada may be labeled as rye, regardless of whether it actually contains the grain.

Outside of that, blenders have a lot of room to play. Most of the bottom-shelf whisky available is light, delicate, and underwhelmingly smooth, like Seagram's 7. But their midrange and premium offerings,

WHISKEY

like Crown Royal's Barrel Select Coffey Rye, Forty Creek's limited-edition releases, and the regular Lot 40, are stunning and boast flavors ranging from banana candy to spicy-sweet vanilla.

IRISH WHISKEY

Despite being the birthplace of whiskey, in 2005, only three distilleries produced whiskey in all of Ireland. Thanks to the craft spirits movement, seven others have opened up since 2006. Although some experts claim that Irish whiskey is distilled three times, it is not true for all producers.

Traditionally, Irish whiskey uses both malted and unmalted barley, sometimes mixed together. There, barley that is malted is usually dried over a coal or wood fire rather than the traditional Scottish peat. It is aged in wood for at least 3 years. Interestingly enough, if a single whiskey is made by mixing together two or more separately distilled batches, it is considered a blended whiskey. The practice is common: Most Irish whiskey (including Jameson) is blended, but Ireland is also producing some immanently sippable single malts like Redbreast 12.

JAPANESE WHISKY

Originally, the art of whisky-making in Japan was aimed at making a product similar to Scotch. Today you can find Japanese single malts and blended whiskies. Although there may be some similarity to Scotch, they tend to have a character all their own.

Although it has been produced since the early 1920s, Japanese whisky has only recently become available within the United States. As it has become more available, its celebrity has also grown: The 2015 edition of *Jim Murray's Whiskey Bible* ranked a whisky from Yamazaki Distillery as the world whiskey of the year. Japanese whiskies are often a bit more expensive, but their light, floral complexity can be a fantastic stepping-stone into enjoying Scotch. To start, pick up a bottle of Hibiki Harmony or Yamazaki 12 for sipping—leave the mixing to other categories.

SCOTCH

Few liquors are quite as polarizing as Scotch. Although the typical flavors vary greatly by region, the peaty, smoky flavor typical of whisky made on the island of Islay seems to be the most iconic. Before fermentation, the barley is allowed to begin sprouting. Then it is dried over peat fires to halt the process. The longer it is dried over a peat fire, the smokier it will be. Once distilled, it is aged for at least 3 years, but it often spends a decade or more in a cask. Though most will rest in a used bourbon barrel, Scotches are also sometimes finished in used sherry, port, or rum casks to give them an extra layer of flavor.

There are five designated official regions in Scotland: Highlands (mild, low to no peat), Lowlands, Campbeltown (which, as of 2016, only has three operational distilleries in existence), Speyside (has the most distilleries), and Islay (some of the peatiest whiskies out there). Though Scotch is also produced on other islands, the regional designation does not apply. For a mild introductory Scotch, pick up Highland Park 12 or Highland Park Dark Origins, but for a bold, peaty alternative, grab an Ardbeg 10-year.

Liqueurs Made from Whiskey

In addition to many bar staples, a surprising number of whiskey producers have begun making whiskey-based liqueurs fairly recently. Some common types include cinnamon whiskies like Fireball or Jim Beam Kentucky Fire and honey whiskies like Jack Daniel's Tennessee Honey or Wild Turkey's American Honey. Newer trends include apple-flavored whiskey like Crown Royal Regal Apple, vanilla, and many others. There is also peach-flavored Southern Comfort, an extremely popular liqueur that has spawned countless shots and many popular drinks, as well as Scotch-based Drambuie and Irish Mist.

Whiskey Tips

Choosing the best possible mixing whiskey will depend on the effect you wish to achieve. For Scotch-based cocktails, a lower-end blend such as Famous Grouse will produce a mild but lightly smoky cocktail. Although you *can* use the good stuff, adding no more than ½ ounce of it will produce the exact same effect—at a much lower cost. For all other whiskey cocktails, choose a product that is neither top shelf nor bottom shelf. In a cocktail, some of the rougher flavors will soften, and it will be better than on its own.

Though some people consider using high-end Scotches or bourbon in cocktails to be sacrilegious, the more important thing to note is that these whiskies are not usually designed to be used in cocktails. An Old Weller Antique 107 Whiskey Sour will likely be more satisfying than one made with Pappy Van Winkle, as the Old Weller is gentler on your wallet and will have more bourbon character.

If you choose to enjoy a whiskey straight, pour it into a tulip-shaped Glencairn, snifter, or bulbous neat glass at room temperature. These vessels are designed to capture aromatic compounds while allowing the harsh alcohol fumes to evaporate. As more and more popular whiskies are sold at barrel proof or cask strength, allowing those fumes to escape can prevent your nose from going numb. To do the same for your taste buds, many experts suggest adding a drop or two of spring water to open up the flavor and aroma.

For the recipes that follow, the type of whiskey specified is taken from the original recipe, where possible, whether it is using rye in a Manhattan (page 217) or Scotch in a Godfather (page 230). Though many other types of whiskey have been used, sometimes interchangeably, in these drinks, we have tried to stick to the historical originals wherever possible.

CLASSIC
WHISKEY COCKTAILS

Manhattan STRONG
COCKTAIL GLASS | COCKTAIL GLASS KNIFE, JIGGER, MIXING GLASS,
BAR SPOON, HAWTHORNE STRAINER

2 ounces rye whiskey
1 ounce sweet vermouth
2 dashes Angostura bitters
1 orange twist or maraschino cherry, for garnish

In a mixing glass, stir all liquid ingredients well with cracked
ice. Strain into in a chilled cocktail glass, garnish with an
orange twist or cherry, and serve.

Blarney Stone: *Substitute Irish whiskey for rye and orange bitters
(store-bought or homemade, page 40) for Angostura.*
Distrito Federal: *Substitute tequila for rye whiskey.*
Rob Roy: *Substitute Scotch for rye whiskey.*
Bobby Burns: *Substitute Scotch for rye whiskey, and add
1 teaspoon Bénédictine.*
Reverse Manhattan: *Use 1 ounce rye whiskey and 2 ounces
sweet vermouth.*

Bronx (a Manhattan variation) STRONG

COCKTAIL GLASS | JIGGER, MIXING GLASS, BAR SPOON,
HAWTHORNE STRAINER

2 ounces gin
1 ounce freshly squeezed orange juice
½ ounce dry vermouth
½ ounce sweet vermouth

Shake all ingredients well with ice, strain into a chilled
cocktail glass, and serve.

Mint Julep STRONG, MINTY

JULEP CUP OR ROCKS GLASS | JIGGER, MUDDLER, BAR SPOON

5 or 6 fresh mint leaves, plus fresh mint leaves from 2 to 4 sprigs,
  for garnish
1 teaspoon Simple Syrup (page 44)
3 ounces bourbon
Straw

Place 5 or 6 mint leaves in the bottom of a chilled julep cup
with Simple Syrup, and lightly bruise. Pack the cup with
crushed ice. Pour bourbon over the ice, and stir until the cup
frosts. Add more ice, and stir again. Garnish with mint and a
straw, and serve.

Georgia Mint Julep: *Substitute 2 ounces Cognac and 1 ounce
peach brandy for bourbon.*
Prescription Julep: *Substitute 1½ ounces Cognac and ½ ounce
rye whiskey for bourbon.*
Champagne Julep: *Substitute ½ ounce Cognac and 3 ounces
champagne for bourbon, and garnish with a lemon peel.*

THE CLASSIC & CRAFT COCKTAIL RECIPE BOOK

Old Fashioned (1880s) STRONG

ROCKS GLASS | KNIFE, JIGGER, MUDDLER, BAR SPOON

½ teaspoon sugar, 1 sugar cube, or 1 teaspoon Simple Syrup
(page 44)
2 or 3 dashes Angostura bitters
1 teaspoon water
2 ounces rye whiskey
1 lemon or orange peel, for garnish
Tiny spoon, for garnish

Place the sugar in the bottom of a chilled rocks glass. Dash the
bitters on top, and add the water. Muddle until the sugar dissolves. Add a large cube of ice, and stir once or twice. Add the
whiskey, stir until chilled, and twist an orange or lemon peel
over the top. Garnish with a tiny spoon, and serve.

Old Fashioned (1950s) FRUITY, STRONG

ROCKS GLASS | KNIFE, JIGGER, MUDDLER, BAR SPOON

1 teaspoon granulated sugar
2 dashes Angostura bitters
1 teaspoon water
1 orange wedge, plus 1 more for garnish
1 maraschino cherry, plus 1 more for garnish
2 ounces bourbon
1 orange or lemon peel, for garnish
Splash club soda

Put the sugar in the bottom of a chilled rocks glass. Dash the
bitters on top, and add the water, orange wedge, and cherry.
Muddle until the sugar dissolves. Add a large cube of ice, and
stir. Add the bourbon, stir again, and twist an orange or lemon
peel over the top. Add a splash of soda water. Garnish with
another orange wedge and maraschino cherry, and serve.

WHISKEY

Sazerac STRONG

ROCKS GLASS | KNIFE, JIGGER, MUDDLER, BAR SPOON

A few dashes absinthe
1 sugar cube or ¼ ounce Simple Syrup (page 44)
2½ ounces rye whiskey
3 dashes Peychaud's bitters
1 lemon twist (see page 49), for garnish

In a chilled rocks glass, add a few drops of absinthe and roll until coated. Pour off the excess. In a second chilled rocks glass, add the Simple Syrup or muddle a sugar cube with a few drops of water. Add a few small ice cubes and the whiskey and bitters. Pour into the absinthe glass, garnish with a lemon twist, and serve.

Vieux Carré STRONG

ROCKS GLASS | JIGGER, MIXING GLASS, BAR SPOON,
HAWTHORNE STRAINER

¾ ounce rye whiskey
¾ ounce Cognac
¾ ounce sweet vermouth
½ teaspoon Bénédictine
1 dash Peychaud's bitters
1 dash Angostura bitters
1 maraschino cherry, for garnish

In a mixing glass, stir all liquid ingredients well with ice. Strain into a chilled rocks glass filled with ice, garnish with a cherry, and serve.

Waldorf Cocktail (a Vieux Carré variation) STRONG

COCKTAIL GLASS | JIGGER, MIXING GLASS, BAR SPOON,
HAWTHORNE STRAINER

¼ ounce absinthe
2 ounces rye whiskey
¾ ounce sweet vermouth
3 or 4 dashes Angostura bitters

Roll the absinthe around in a mixing glass until coated, and
discard the excess. Add the remaining ingredients and ice, and
stir well. Strain into a chilled cocktail glass, and serve.

Whiskey Sour CITRUSY

COUPE GLASS OR SOUR GLASS | JIGGER, SHAKER,
HAWTHORNE STRAINER

2 ounces bourbon
1 ounce freshly squeezed lemon juice
1 ounce Simple Syrup (page 44)
1 maraschino cherry, for garnish (optional)

Shake all liquid ingredients well with cracked ice, and strain
into a chilled cocktail glass or sour glass. Garnish with the
cherry (if using), and serve.

Boston Sour: *Add egg white, shake without ice first, and then
shake with ice.*
Dizzy Sour: *Add 3 dashes Bénédictine, reduce whiskey by ½ ounce,
and float ½ to 1 ounce of Jamaica rum on top (see page 57).*
Hari Kari: *Mix in a chilled Collins glass, top with soda water, and
garnish with whatever fruit you might have.*
New York Sour: *Float ½ ounce fruity red wine on top (see
page 57).*

CRAFT
WHISKEY COCKTAILS

Algonquin FRUITY, TART
COCKTAIL GLASS | KNIFE, JIGGER, MIXING GLASS, BAR SPOON, HAWTHORNE STRAINER

1½ ounces rye whiskey
¾ ounce sweet vermouth
¾ ounce pineapple juice
1 orange peel, for garnish

In a mixing glass, stir all liquid ingredients well with ice (you can shake, but the pineapple juice will foam). Strain into a chilled cocktail glass, garnish with the orange peel, and serve.

Bayou Bash SWEET, FRUITY
Court of Two Sisters, New Orleans

COLLINS GLASS | KNIFE, JIGGER, SHAKER

1¼ ounces Southern Comfort liqueur
1 ounce freshly squeezed orange juice
¾ ounce pineapple juice
¼ ounce grenadine (store-bought or homemade, page 45)
¾ ounce cherry juice
1¼ ounces sweet-and-sour mix
¾ ounce red wine, for topping
½ orange slice, for garnish
1 cherry on a frill pick, for garnish

THE CLASSIC & CRAFT COCKTAIL RECIPE BOOK

Shake all liquid ingredients except the red wine well with ice, and pour into a chilled Collins glass. Top with the red wine, garnish with the orange slice and cherry pick, and serve.

Blackthorn STRONG

COCKTAIL GLASS | KNIFE, JIGGER, MIXING GLASS, BAR SPOON, HAWTHORNE STRAINER

2 ounces Irish whiskey
1 ounce sweet vermouth
2 dashes Angostura bitters
1 dash absinthe
1 lemon twist (see page 49), for garnish

In a mixing glass, stir all liquid ingredients well with ice. Strain into a chilled cocktail glass, garnish with a lemon twist, and serve.

Blinker TART, FRUITY

COCKTAIL GLASS | KNIFE, JIGGER, SHAKER, HAWTHORNE STRAINER

2 ounces rye whiskey
½ ounce freshly squeezed white grapefruit juice (not pink)
1 teaspoon to ½ ounce raspberry syrup or grenadine
  (store-bought or homemade, page 45), to taste
1 grapefruit twist (see page 49), for garnish

Shake all liquid ingredients vigorously with ice. Strain into a chilled cocktail glass, garnish with the grapefruit twist, and serve.

Blood and Sand SMOKY, SWEET

COUPE OR COCKTAIL GLASS | KNIFE, JIGGER, SHAKER,
HAWTHORNE STRAINER

¾ ounce Scotch
¾ ounce sweet vermouth
¾ ounce Cherry Heering
¾ ounce freshly squeezed orange juice
1 orange peel, for garnish

Shake all liquid ingredients well with ice, and strain into a
chilled coupe or cocktail glass. Garnish with the orange peel,
and serve.

Bourbon Iced Tea TEA, MINTY

COLLINS GLASS | KNIFE, JIGGER, SHAKER, HAWTHORNE STRAINER

4 ounces iced tea
2 ounces bourbon
2 ounces Honey Mint Syrup*
½ ounce freshly squeezed lemon juice
Lemon wedge, for garnish

Shake all liquid ingredients well with ice. Strain into a chilled
Collins glass filled with ice, garnish with a lemon wedge,
and serve.

*Honey Mint Syrup: Infuse Honey Syrup (page 44) with 2 or 3 fresh
mint sprigs.*

THE CLASSIC & CRAFT COCKTAIL RECIPE BOOK

Bourbon Renewal CITRUSY, FRESH

 Jeffrey Morgenthaler, Portland, Oregon

ROCKS GLASS | KNIFE, JIGGER, SHAKER, HAWTHORNE STRAINER

2 ounces bourbon
1 ounce freshly squeezed lemon juice
½ ounce crème de cassis
½ ounce Simple Syrup (page 44)
1 dash Angostura bitters
1 lemon wedge, for garnish

Shake all liquid ingredients with ice, and strain into a chilled rocks glass full of ice. Garnish with a lemon wedge, and serve.

Brooklyn STRONG

COCKTAIL GLASS | JIGGER, MIXING GLASS, BAR SPOON,
HAWTHORNE STRAINER

2 ounces rye or other whiskey
1 ounce dry vermouth
¼ ounce maraschino cherry liqueur, preferably Luxardo
¼ ounce Amer Picon, or a few dashes Angostura or orange bitters
  (store-bought or homemade, page 40)

In a mixing glass, stir all ingredients well with ice. Strain into a chilled cocktail glass, and serve.

Brown Derby TART, CITRUSY

COCKTAIL GLASS | JIGGER, SHAKER, HAWTHORNE STRAINER

2 ounces bourbon
1 ounce grapefruit juice
½ ounce Honey Syrup (page 44)

Shake all ingredients with ice until chilled, strain into a chilled cocktail glass, and serve.

Bufala Negra FRESH, SPICY
Jerry Slater, Atlanta

ROCKS GLASS | JIGGER, SHAKER, MUDDLER, HAWTHORNE STRAINER

½ ounce Balsamic Syrup*
4 fresh basil leaves, plus 1 more for garnish
1 brown sugar cube
1½ ounces bourbon
2 ounces ginger beer, for topping

In a cocktail shaker, muddle the first 3 ingredients. Add the bourbon and ice, and shake hard. Strain over fresh ice cubes into a chilled rocks glass. Top with ginger beer, garnish with an additional basil leaf, and serve.

*Balsamic Syrup: Combine ¼ cup balsamic vinegar and ¼ cup Simple Syrup (page 44) in a saucepan over medium-high heat. Bring just to a boil, reduce heat to medium-low, and let simmer for 1 minute, stirring occasionally. Remove from heat and let cool. Makes ½ cup.

Canadian Cocktail STRONG
ROCKS GLASS | JIGGER, SHAKER, HAWTHORNE STRAINER

2 ounces Canadian whisky
½ ounce Cointreau
1 teaspoon Simple Syrup (page 44)
2 dashes Angostura bitters

Shake all ingredients with ice. Strain into a chilled rocks glass full of ice, and serve.

Chancellor STRONG
COCKTAIL GLASS | JIGGER, MIXING GLASS, BAR SPOON,
HAWTHORNE STRAINER

2 ounces blended Scotch
1 ounce ruby port
½ ounce French vermouth
2 dashes orange bitters (store-bought or homemade, page 40)

In a mixing glass, stir all ingredients well with cracked ice.
Strain into a chilled cocktail glass and serve.

Churchill Downs Cooler SPICY, STRONG
COLLINS GLASS | JIGGER, BAR SPOON

1½ ounces bourbon
1 ounce brandy
½ ounce Triple Sec
4 ounces ginger ale, for topping

In a chilled Collins glass full of ice, mix first 3 ingredients.
Top with the ginger ale, stir gently, and serve.

Cocktail de la Louisiane STRONG, SWEET
COCKTAIL GLASS | JIGGER, MIXING GLASS, BAR SPOON,
HAWTHORNE STRAINER

¾ ounce rye whiskey
¾ ounce Bénédictine
¾ ounce sweet vermouth
3 dashes Herbsaint or absinthe
3 dashes Peychaud's bitters
1 maraschino cherry, for garnish

In a mixing glass, stir all liquid ingredients with cracked ice. Strain into a chilled cocktail glass, garnish with the cherry, and serve.

Democrat CITRUSY

 Jon Santer, San Francisco

COLLINS GLASS | KNIFE, JIGGER, BAR SPOON

2 ounces bourbon
¾ ounce freshly squeezed lemon juice
½ ounce peach liqueur
½ ounce Honey Syrup (page 44)
1 lemon wheel (see page 49), for garnish

In a chilled Collins glass, stir all liquid ingredients with crushed ice until cold. Add more ice, garnish with the lemon wheel, and serve.

Derby CITRUSY

COCKTAIL GLASS | KNIFE, JIGGER, SHAKER, HAWTHORNE STRAINER

1 ounce bourbon
¾ ounce freshly squeezed lime juice
½ ounce sweet vermouth
½ ounce Grand Marnier or dry Curaçao
1 lime wedge or fresh mint leaf, for garnish

Shake all liquid ingredients well with ice, and strain into a chilled cocktail glass. Garnish with the lime wedge or mint leaf, and serve.

THE CLASSIC & CRAFT COCKTAIL RECIPE BOOK

Dry County Cocktail DRY, SPICY

Jonny Raglin, San Francisco

COUPE GLASS | KNIFE, JIGGER, MIXING GLASS, BAR SPOON,
HAWTHORNE STRAINER

2 ounces Tennessee whiskey
¾ ounce dry vermouth
½ ounce Ginger Syrup (page 45)
1 dash lemon bitters
1 lemon twist (see page 49), for garnish

Fill a mixing glass with ice. Add all ingredients except the
lemon twist, and stir well. Strain into a chilled coupe, garnish
with the lemon twist, and serve.

Expat CITRUSY, STRONG

Lauren Schell, Little Branch, New York

COUPE GLASS | JIGGER, SHAKER, HAWTHORNE STRAINER

2 ounces bourbon
1 ounce freshly squeezed lime juice
¾ ounce Simple Syrup (page 44)
2 dashes Angostura bitters
1 fresh mint leaf, for garnish

Shake all liquid ingredients with ice, and strain into a chilled
coupe. Garnish with the mint leaf, and serve.

Glasgow STRONG

COCKTAIL GLASS | JIGGER, MIXING GLASS, BAR SPOON,
HAWTHORNE STRAINER

2 ounces blended Scotch
1 ounce dry vermouth
1 teaspoon absinthe
1 dash Peychaud's bitters

In a mixing glass, stir all ingredients well with cracked ice.
Strain into a chilled cocktail glass, get creative with your
garnish, and serve.

Godfather STRONG

ROCKS GLASS | JIGGER, MIXING GLASS, BAR SPOON,
HAWTHORNE STRAINER

2 ounces Scotch or bourbon
½ ounce amaretto

In a mixing glass, stir both ingredients well with ice. Strain
into a chilled rocks glass full of ice, and serve.

Goldrush CITRUSY

DOUBLE ROCKS GLASS | JIGGER, SHAKER, HAWTHORNE STRAINER

2 ounces bourbon
1 ounce freshly squeezed lemon juice
1 ounce Honey Syrup (page 44)

Shake all ingredients well with ice, strain into a chilled double
rocks glass full of ice, and serve.

Goonies Never Say Die! STRONG, TROPICAL, SPICY

Julian Goglia, The Pinewood, Atlanta

ROCKS GLASS | JIGGER, SHAKER, HAWTHORNE STRAINER

1½ ounces bourbon
½ ounce falernum, preferably Taylor's Velvet Falernum*
½ ounce freshly squeezed lime juice
½ ounce Ginger Syrup (page 45)
1 piece candied ginger, for garnish (optional)
Grains of paradise,** for garnish (optional)

Shake all liquid ingredients well with ice, and strain over ice into a chilled rocks glass. Garnish with a candied ginger chunk and grains of paradise, if desired, and serve.

See page 158 for more on Velvet Falernum.
**Commonly known as ossame, or grains of paradise, this spice has a pungent, peppery flavor.*

Gray Wolf STRONG

Julia Momose, GreenRiver, Chicago

DOUBLE ROCKS GLASS | KNIFE, JIGGER, MIXING GLASS, BAR SPOON, HAWTHORNE STRAINER

2 ounces Yamazaki 12-Year Japanese whisky
¼ ounce Demerara Syrup (page 44)
½ teaspoon plum vinegar
½ teaspoon Bénédictine
2 dashes Angostura bitters
1 grapefruit twist (see page 49), for garnish

In a mixing glass, stir all liquid ingredients well with ice. Strain into a chilled double rocks glass over one big ice cube. Garnish with the grapefruit twist, discard the peel, and serve.

Highlander STRONG

Paul Harrington, Spokane*

COCKTAIL GLASS | KNIFE, JIGGER, MIXING GLASS, BAR SPOON,
HAWTHORNE STRAINER

2 ounces Scotch
½ ounce Bénédictine
1 dash Angostura bitters
1 lemon twist (see page 49), for garnish

In a mixing glass, stir the first 3 ingredients well with ice.
Strain into a chilled cocktail glass, garnish with the lemon
twist, and serve.

*Reprinted with permission from Cocktail: The Drinks Bible for the
21st Century.

Horse's Neck (With a Kick) SWEET

HIGHBALL GLASS OR COLLINS GLASS | CHANNEL KNIFE, JIGGER,
BAR SPOON

1 lemon spiral (see page 49), for garnish
2 ounces bourbon
3 dashes Angostura bitters
Ginger ale, for topping

Drop the lemon spiral gently into a chilled highball or Collins
glass, leaving one end hanging over the lip. Fill the glass
with ice, and add bourbon and bitters. Top with ginger ale,
and serve.

THE CLASSIC & CRAFT COCKTAIL RECIPE BOOK

Improved Whiskey Cocktail STRONG

ROCKS GLASS | KNIFE, JIGGER, MIXING GLASS, BAR SPOON,
HAWTHORNE STRAINER

2 ounces bourbon or rye
1 teaspoon Simple Syrup (page 44)
1 teaspoon maraschino cherry liqueur
1 dash Angostura bitters
1 dash Peychaud's bitters
1 dash absinthe
1 lemon or orange peel, for garnish

In a mixing glass, stir all liquid ingredients well with ice.
Strain into a chilled rocks glass, garnish with a lemon or
orange peel, and serve.

Indian Summer STRONG

Jared Schubert, Louisville, Kentucky

ROCKS GLASS | KNIFE, JIGGER, MIXING GLASS, BAR SPOON,
HAWTHORNE STRAINER, ZESTER OR GRATER

1½ ounces Michter's bourbon
½ ounce Cantaloupe Syrup*
2 dashes Angostura bitters
1 lemon peel, for garnish
Shaved cantaloupe, for garnish

In a mixing glass, stir all liquid ingredients well with ice.
Strain into a chilled rocks glass filled with ice. Garnish with
the lemon peel and shaved cantaloupe, and serve.

*Cantaloupe Syrup: Boil 1 cup water and 1 cup sugar together, add-
ing a half a cubed cantaloupe. Reduce heat to simmer. When you can
smell it from another room, it is ready.*

Irish Redhead SWEET

HIGHBALL GLASS | KNIFE, JIGGER, BAR SPOON

3 ounces Irish whiskey
1 ounce grenadine (store-bought or homemade, page 45)
1 squeeze of a lemon wedge
1 squeeze of a lime wedge
5 to 6 ounces lemon-lime soda, such as Sprite
1 lemon or lime wedge, for garnish

Pour the whiskey, grenadine, and citrus juice into a chilled highball glass filled with ice. Fill with lemon-lime soda, garnish with the lemon or lime wedge, and serve.

Lion's Tail CITRUSY

COCKTAIL OR COUPE GLASS | JIGGER, SHAKER, HAWTHORNE STRAINER

2 ounces bourbon
½ ounce pimento dram
½ ounce freshly squeezed lime juice
1 teaspoon gomme syrup
1 dash Angostura bitters

Shake all ingredients well with ice, strain into a chilled cocktail or coupe glass, and serve.

Millionaire CREAMY, STRONG

COCKTAIL GLASS | JIGGER, SHAKER, HAWTHORNE STRAINER, FINE STRAINER

2 ounces rye whisky
½ ounce Grand Marnier
1 dash grenadine (store-bought or homemade, page 45)
1 egg white

THE CLASSIC & CRAFT COCKTAIL RECIPE BOOK

Add all ingredients to a cocktail shaker, adding egg white last. Shake vigorously without ice, and then add ice and shake well again. Double strain into a chilled cocktail glass, and serve.

Native New Yorker STRONG

Gates Otsuji, The Standard, New York City

COUPE GLASS | JIGGER, MIXING GLASS, BAR SPOON, HAWTHORNE STRAINER

¼ ounce Johnnie Walker Double Black
2 ounces Parce 12-Year Colombian rum
¾ ounce Lustau manzanilla sherry
¼ ounce Amargo-Vallet bitter liqueur
¼ ounce Rich Demerara Syrup (page 44)

Pour the Johnnie Walker Double Black into a chilled coupe. Roll the glass to coat the inside, and pour out the extra. In a mixing glass, stir the remaining ingredients with ice until chilled through. Strain into the coupe glass, and serve.

New York Cocktail CITRUSY, TART

COCKTAIL GLASS | KNIFE, JIGGER, SHAKER, HAWTHORNE STRAINER

2 ounces Rittenhouse rye
½ ounce freshly squeezed lime juice
½ ounce Simple Syrup (page 44)
1 teaspoon grenadine (store-bought or homemade, page 45)
1 orange peel, for garnish

Shake all liquid ingredients well with ice, and strain into a chilled cocktail glass. Garnish with the orange peel, and serve.

WHISKEY

Old Pal STRONG, DRY

COCKTAIL GLASS | KNIFE, JIGGER, MIXING GLASS, BAR SPOON,
HAWTHORNE STRAINER

1½ ounces bourbon or rye whiskey
¾ ounce dry vermouth
¾ ounce Campari liqueur
1 lemon twist (see page 49), for garnish

In a mixing glass, stir all liquid ingredients well with ice.
Strain into a chilled cocktail glass, garnish with the lemon
twist, and serve.

Oriental Cocktail STRONG, CITRUSY

COCKTAIL GLASS | KNIFE, JIGGER, SHAKER, HAWTHORNE STRAINER,
FINE STRAINER

1½ ounces rye whiskey
¾ ounce Cointreau
¾ ounce sweet vermouth
½ ounce freshly squeezed lime juice
1 orange twist (see page 49), for garnish

Shake all liquid ingredients well with ice, and then double
strain into a chilled cocktail glass. Garnish with the orange
twist, and serve.

Pappy Old Fashioned Jell-O Shots STRONG

◀ *Jeremy Johnson, Meta, Louisville, Kentucky*

15 TO 20 (1-OUNCE) PLASTIC SHOT GLASSES | TRAY, BOWL, PITCHER, BAR SPOON, SAUCEPAN

MAKES 15 TO 20 SHOTS

Unflavored nonstick cooking spray
15 to 20 brandied cherries
1½ cups Pappy Van Winkle (15- or 12-Year) bourbon
½ cup water
¼ cup Demerara Syrup (page 44)
6 dashes Angostura bitters
3 packets gelatin

Lightly coat the shot glasses with the cooking spray, and place them on a tray or baking sheet. Drop a brandied cherry into each. In a pitcher, stir to combine the liquid ingredients. Leave half in the pitcher, and heat the other half in a saucepan over medium-low heat until steaming, but not boiling. Remove from the heat, and rapidly stir in the gelatin. Pour the heated gelatin mixture into the pitcher of room-temperature liquid, and stir to combine. Pour into the prepared shot glasses, chill the tray in the refrigerator for about 2 hours, and serve.

A word of advice: Wash your saucepan and pitcher immediately after pouring the shots, before the mixture cements itself to them.

Preakness Cocktail STRONG, SWEET

COCKTAIL GLASS | KNIFE, JIGGER, MIXING GLASS, BAR SPOON,
HAWTHORNE STRAINER

1½ ounces rye whiskey
¾ ounce sweet vermouth
¼ ounce Bénédictine
1 dash Angostura bitters
1 lemon twist (see page 49), for garnish

In a mixing glass, stir all liquid ingredients well with ice.
Strain into a chilled cocktail glass, garnish with a lemon twist,
and serve.

Presbyterian SMOKY, SWEET

COLLINS GLASS | JIGGER

2 ounces Scotch or bourbon or rye whiskey
Ginger ale, for topping
Club soda, for topping

Pour the Scotch into a chilled Collins glass, and fill with ice.
Top with equal amounts of ginger ale and soda, and serve.

Remember the Maine STRONG, SWEET

COCKTAIL GLASS | JIGGER, MIXING GLASS, BAR SPOON,
HAWTHORNE STRAINER

2 ounces rye whiskey
¾ ounce sweet vermouth
2 teaspoons Cherry Heering
½ teaspoon absinthe or absinthe substitute such as Pernod
1 maraschino cherry, for garnish

In a mixing glass, stir all liquid ingredients well with ice. Strain into a chilled cocktail glass, garnish with the cherry, and serve.

Revolver STRONG, COFFEE
COCKTAIL GLASS | KNIFE, JIGGER, MIXING GLASS, BAR SPOON, HAWTHORNE STRAINER

2 ounces bourbon
½ ounce coffee liqueur
2 dashes orange bitters (store-bought or homemade, page 40)
1 orange twist (see page 49), for garnish

In a mixing glass, stir all liquid ingredients well with ice. Strain into a chilled cocktail glass, garnish with the orange twist, and serve.

Rickey STRONG, TART
HIGHBALL GLASS | JIGGER, BAR SPOON

½ lime
1½ ounces bourbon
Club soda, for topping

Squeeze the lime into a chilled highball glass filled with ice, drop in the spent shell, and add the bourbon. Top with club soda, stir briefly to combine, and serve.

Rusty Nail STRONG
DOUBLE ROCKS GLASS | JIGGER, BAR SPOON

2 ounces blended Scotch
½ ounce Drambuie liqueur

Pour both ingredients into a chilled double rocks glass. Fill with ice, stir, and serve.

Scofflaw STRONG, CITRUSY
COCKTAIL GLASS | KNIFE, JIGGER, SHAKER, HAWTHORNE STRAINER

1½ ounces rye whiskey
1 ounce dry vermouth
¾ ounce freshly squeezed lime juice
½ ounce grenadine (store-bought or homemade, page 45)
1 dash orange bitters (store-bought or homemade, page 40)
1 orange twist (see page 49), for garnish (optional)

Shake all liquid ingredients well with ice, and strain into a chilled cocktail glass. Garnish, if you so choose, with the orange twist, and serve.

Sea Captain's Special STRONG, BUBBLY
ROCKS GLASS | JIGGER, MUDDLER

1 sugar cube, or ½ teaspoon sugar
3 dashes Angostura bitters
Splash water or club soda
2½ ounces rye whisky
Brut champagne, for topping
2 dashes absinthe, for topping

Put the sugar in a chilled rocks glass. Dash the bitters directly onto the sugar, and add a small splash of water or soda. Crush the sugar with a muddler, and swirl the glass to coat it evenly. Add a large ice cube, and pour in the whiskey. Top with the champagne and absinthe, and serve.

Smokescreen FRESH, SMOKY

 *Alex Day, Los Angeles*

DOUBLE ROCKS GLASS | JIGGER, SHAKER, MUDDLER,
HAWTHORNE STRAINER

4 fresh mint leaves, plus leaves of 1 fresh mint sprig, for garnish
1½ ounces Scotch, preferably Bowmore Legend Islay Scotch
¾ ounce freshly squeezed lime juice
¾ ounce Simple Syrup (page 44)
¼ ounce green Chartreuse

Drop the mint leaves into a cocktail shaker, and lightly bruise
using the muddler. Add all liquid ingredients, and shake well
with ice. Strain into a chilled double rocks glass with 1 large
ice cube, garnish with the mint leaves, and serve.

Suburban STRONG

COCKTAIL GLASS | JIGGER, MIXING GLASS, BAR SPOON,
HAWTHORNE STRAINER

1½ ounces rye whisky
½ ounce dark rum
½ ounce port
1 dash orange bitters (store-bought or homemade, page 40)
1 dash Angostura bitters

In a mixing glass, stir all ingredients well with cracked ice.
Strain into a chilled cocktail glass, and serve.

Suffering Bastard STRONG, CITRUSY

ROCKS GLASS | JIGGER

1 ounce bourbon
1 ounce gin
1 ounce freshly squeezed lime juice
1 dash Angostura bitters
4 ounces chilled ginger ale, for topping
1 fresh mint sprig or orange slice, for garnish

Pour the first 4 ingredients into a chilled rocks glass filled with ice. Top with ginger ale, add ice if needed, garnish, and serve.

Toronto STRONG, BITTER

COCKTAIL GLASS | KNIFE, JIGGER, MIXING GLASS, BAR SPOON, HAWTHORNE STRAINER

2 ounces rye whiskey
¼ ounce Fernet Branca
¼ ounce Simple Syrup (page 44)
2 dashes Angostura bitters
1 orange peel, for garnish

In a mixing glass, stir the liquid ingredients well with cracked ice. Strain into a chilled cocktail glass. Squeeze a piece of orange peel over the drink, drop it in, and serve.

THE CLASSIC & CRAFT COCKTAIL RECIPE BOOK

Velveteen STRONG, TROPICAL

Gregory Fellows, Annisa, New York City

CORDIAL GLASS | JIGGER, MIXING GLASS, BAR SPOON,
HAWTHORNE STRAINER

2 ounces Russell's rye
¾ ounce green Chartreuse
¾ ounce John D. Taylor's Velvet Falernum
½ ounce freshly squeezed lemon juice
4 drops Peychaud's bitters, for garnish

In a mixing glass, stir the first 4 ingredients gently with
ice. Strain into a chilled cordial glass, finish with 4 drops
Peychaud's bitters, and serve.

Ward Eight CITRUSY, FRUITY

COCKTAIL GLASS | JIGGER, SHAKER, HAWTHORNE STRAINER

2 ounces rye whisky
¾ ounce freshly squeezed lemon juice
¾ ounce freshly squeezed orange juice
1 teaspoon to ½ ounce grenadine (store-bought or homemade,
   page 45), to taste

Shake all ingredients well with ice, strain into a chilled
cocktail glass, and serve.

Whiskey Slush FRUITY

COLLINS GLASSES | KNIFE, LARGE PLASTIC PITCHER, LARGE SPOON, BAR SPOON

SERVES 15 TO 20

7 cups water
1 (12-ounce) can frozen lemonade concentrate
1 (6-ounce) can frozen orange juice concentrate
2 cups strong brewed black tea
2 cups whiskey
1 cup white sugar
1 (1-liter) bottle ginger ale soda, for topping
2 lemons cut into wedges, for garnish

In a large plastic pitcher, stir to combine all ingredients except the ginger ale and lemon wedges. Mix well and freeze for 24 hours. Pour or spoon into chilled Collins glasses, filling them three-quarters full. Top each glass with ginger ale, stir, garnish each with a lemon wedge, and serve.

CHAPTER ELEVEN

WINE, FORTIFIED WINE & BEER

This book focuses mainly on cocktails made with distilled liquors. But there are a few fermented ingredients that every spirit-lover should know. Beer and wine are fermented alcoholic beverages made from grain and fruit, respectively. Fortified wine is simply wine with brandy or neutral grain spirit added to increase the alcohol content, and sometimes spices and herbs to improve the flavor. The diversity within these three categories is staggering. As a result, this section includes only the most common types of wine and beer, and some of the fortified wines used frequently in cocktails or sipped straight.

AS YOU WILL FIND BELOW, wines are typically classified by the type of grape pressed and fermented to make them, also known as their varietal. Champagne and sparkling wines, which tend to be some of the most recognizable, are used in cocktails more often than others. As a result, these wines have their own chapter on page 95. Beers are not as commonly used in cocktails as wines or wine-based products but are classified by the type of malt and hops used to make them, as well as the resulting flavor profile. Classifying fortified wines tends to be slightly easier, as most are defined by where they're produced in addition to how.

Types of Wine

REDS

Red blends: Though blended wine is produced all over the world, Bordeaux red blends are one of the most copied styles in the world. These wines tend to be big, bold, earthy, and fruity with tiny hints of oak.

Cabernet franc: Cabernet franc grapes are often used in blending Bordeaux and the United States take on the style called *Meritage*. It is also available as a varietal on its own and tends to be earthier than its better-known cousin, cabernet sauvignon. Experts also describe it as having coffee and blueberry notes, along with some vegetal green pepper ones.

Cabernet sauvignon: The cabernet sauvignon grape is probably the grape that defines most wine from the California Napa Valley. When grown elsewhere in the world, this grape often develops a very different flavor profile and is more commonly used in blends. California cabs tend to be fruity, with lots of black cherry, currant, and oaky notes, but elsewhere, it tends toward being more vegetal.

Malbec: In the prominent French wine region of Bordeaux, Malbec is usually left for blending in small quantities. But Argentinian malbecs tend to spicy and bold, and often improve with some time in a barrel.

Merlot: Merlot is one of the easiest reds to like, drink, and remember. It is often considered to be the chardonnay of reds. In the 1990s, it was quite popular as a varietal wine, but its fame also inspired a variety of mediocre products. For the best merlots, look for one produced in Bordeaux or Washington State.

Pinot noir: For winemakers, pinot noir grapes are some of the most challenging to grow. They are often used in champagnes and other sparkling wines. When ripened, the grapes can produce a jammy, dense wine on their own. Though Burgundy's pinot noir is considered the standard, some producers in Oregon and California also make delicious, varied varietals with a huge variety of flavor profiles.

Syrah: Known as shiraz in Australia, syrah has become a popular grape in California and Washington for its spiciness and slight pepperiness. Australian shiraz wines range from light and fruity to dense and rich and are also made into sparkling and fortified products. As with most wines, the most striking expressions of this wine are produced in France. Made in the northern Rhône, the best syrah is incredibly complex wine that still features spice and pepper and can age for decades.

Zinfandel: Originally, zinfandel was California's signature grape. Now, it is grown all over the world, and its lineage has been traced to Croatia. Within California, varietals vary widely depending on where they are grown. Typically, it has notes of jam, pepper, and red berries. The grape is also used for white zinfandel, which accounts for about 85 percent of all zinfandel wines and is often the first wine drinkers try.

WHITES

Chardonnay: Like merlot, chardonnay is one of the most diverse and widely planted grapes. Oak-aged wines made with the grape tend to be buttery, but unaged versions appeal to lovers of crisp, citrusy wines. It

WINE, FORTIFIED WINE & BEER

is used in wines ranging from luxury blanc de blanc champagnes (see page 97) to rich, oily, smooth still wines.

Moscato: This wine is famous for its sweetness and bright fruit flavors including peach, orange blossom, and nectarine. Most moscatos are slightly bubbly, with a distinctive aroma. They tend to have a lower alcohol content than many other wines and are made from muscat blanc grapes. Grown all over the world, this grape is believed by some to be the oldest cultivated strain. Really the only difference between moscato and pink moscato is that the pink version has red wine, often merlot, added for color.

Pinot gris: Though there is much confusion about the differences between pinot gris and pinot grigio, the two terms are France and Italy's names, respectively, for the same grape. It is significant in both countries, along with the Pacific Northwest United States. As with any wine, where the grapes are grown determines the exact flavors. Here, they usually range from citrusy lime to nectarine. Italian versions tend to be dry, with a good bit of acidity, while French pinot gris has a faint note of honey. The American take tends to be fruitier and less acidic, but many wines from the Pacific Northwest can be quite high in acid content.

Riesling: This aromatic, refreshing white tends to have a variety of fruit flavors and is sold in a tall, skinny bottle. It is usually quite crisp but is best known for its strong floral aroma. Though it has the reputation for being a sweet wine, most rieslings have a only touch of sweetness, and some are very dry indeed. The sweetness ranges, but many producers are now using a dryness scale on the bottle. Typically, wines with lower alcohol content will be sweeter.

Sauvignon blanc: This grape also goes by the name *fumé blanc*, and flavor-wise it tends to be distinctively different from most other whites. The name translates to "wild white," and the flavors in this varietal tend to be herbal and green with some grapefruit. Wines made from this grape fall on a wide spectrum of flavors ranging from limey, from unripened grapes, to the flavor of white peach in the ripened ones. Most tend to be on the dry side, but some producers in New Zealand and California leave a couple of grams of residual sugar.

Rosé: Unlike reds and whites, rosé isn't made with a specific grape varietal. Its color comes from leaving the skins of red grapes in the fermenting juice for a short time—sometimes only a few hours. The winemaker closely controls the color of the wine and will remove the skins when it reaches the ideal tone. This process is done three ways: by maceration, where the entire batch is made into rosé; *saignée* or bled, where some of the juice is removed to make rosé and the rest will be red; and blending, where a bit of red wine is added to a vat of white wine. Blending is the least common but happens more with sparkling wine. Taste-wise, red fruit, unripe fruit, citrus, and flowers tend to be the dominant rosé tastes.

Fruit wine: As with brandies, any fruit that can be fermented can be used to make wine. But wines that aren't made from grapes are considered fruit wines and are usually referred to by their primary ingredients. One of the most popular is apple wine, which is better known as cider. In Japan, China, Korea, and Taiwan, plum wine is very common, and it is produced in a variety of styles. The Southern United States produces a good deal of muscadine wine. From most fruit wines, expect a strong fruit character and a sweetness that depends on the sugar content of the fruit used in fermentation.

Types of Fortified Wine

Port: Produced exclusively in the Douro Valley in northern Portugal, *porto*, or port, comes in varieties ranging from sweet red to dry white. Port tends to be richer and sweeter than unfortified wines. To make port, a grape-based, brandy-like spirit is added to wine before it ferments fully, and it tends to be around 19 to 20 percent alcohol by volume. Port is available in different varieties including ruby, rose, white, and tawny, the most common.

Sherry: In the cocktail world, sherry may be the most historically famous of the fortified wines for its role in early cocktails like the

Sherry Cobbler (page 259). Made in Andalusia, Spain, about a half dozen varieties exist. Sherry is produced by adding brandy after the fermentation process has ended. Since the product is quite dry, sweetness is added later. The liquid then goes through the solera method, which moves portions of the sherry through a series of barrels of gradually older wines. These barrels are never entirely emptied, so some part of the resulting blend may be quite old. Sherries vary in minimum age requirements and alcohol content, depending on their style, and are incredibly varied in taste from rich amontillados and finos to drier moscatels and undrinkable blended cream sherries made for cooking.

Madeira: Hailing from Portugal's Madeira Islands, this fortified wine accounted for some of the first wine imported into the United States. Varieties range from dry to sweet, and madeira is best known for its aging process. Called *estufagem,* this process of heating, aging, oxidation, and mild pasteurization can be produced either in months with a series of hot water tanks or steam or naturally over a few decades. It is now required for a product to be legally called madeira.

Marsala: Located on the Italian island of Sicily, the city of Marsala produces fortified wines that range from 15 to 20 percent alcohol by volume. It is classified by age, color, and sweetness level, and the styles run from dry aperitifs to sweet dessert wines.

Vermouth: Technically, vermouth is part of a subset of fortified wines called aromatized wine. Vermouth has been around since the time of the ancient Greeks and is made in two different styles: sweet, also called Italian vermouth, and dry, sometimes called French vermouth. But the country designations no longer hold, as both types are produced in both Italy and France. In terms of cocktails, vermouth is usually used as an auxiliary ingredient rather than taking a main role, but it can also be sipped by itself.

Types of Beer

Only two overarching categories of beer are produced in the world: lagers and ales. The difference between the two is the type of yeast used during fermentation: Lagers use yeast that ferments at the bottom, while ales use so-called top-fermenting yeast. Lagers tend to be smooth and clean, without fruitiness.

Amber ale: Amber ales can vary widely but range from quite hoppy to hugely malty. Created as a variation of the American pale ale, these beers vary by region. They're often sweeter than pale ales.

Barleywine: Barleywines are rich, strong ales that range in color from amber to copper. They're intended to be savored and sipped like fine wines. Barleywines are often flavored with hops along with a strong dose of caramel maltiness. These assertive beers have a rich mouthfeel.

Belgian dubbel: Dubbels tend to be malty and rich, with a lot of dark fruit notes. These deep copper ales tend to be medium-bodied and have moderate levels of carbonation, but despite the alcohol content, they don't taste strongly of it.

Belgian tripel: These complex, dry, and spicy beers may have banana notes but definitely have a high alcohol content—around 10 percent ABV. They, too, tend to be moderately carbonated, and most of them have a rich gold color.

Brown ale: This category of beer overarches the American and British brown ales. Generally, they tend to have caramel flavor and a dose of sweetness with a very mild hoppiness. Easily drinkable, this style also encompasses dark ales, along with a pretty large spectrum of food-friendly beers.

IPA: Though IPA stands for *India pale ale*, it is never spelled out because these beers never went to India, and some aren't pale. Typically, these beers are quite bitter and citrusy, but with little to no sweetness. The range of citrus flavors varies based on the exact types of hops used in that beer's production.

Pale ale: Most countries with a history of brewing beer have distinctive pale ales. This type of beer is typically a light straw color and has a more accessible balance of flavors than an IPA.

Pilsner: This style of beer originated in the Czech Republic with Pilsner Urquell, which is the only beer that can be labeled as a pilsner in that country. This type of beer tends to be lighter in color, with a prominent bitter flavor and crisp character. Some of the most popular so-called domestic beers are made in this style, but many craft pilsners are also available.

Porter: Though porters are different than stouts, no singular definition of the defining characteristics between the two exists. Historically, stouts are the strongest porters, and they were originally called stout porters. Nowadays, the main difference is in the malt used to brew each: Most porters are made from malted barley, while stouts are primarily made from unmalted barley. But the rule is by no means hard or fast.

Saison: Also known as farmhouse ale or bière de garde, this rustic style encompasses a huge variety of beers. Usually, saisons are highly carbonated and slightly bitter, but they range in alcohol content, color, and flavor profile. Others have a distinct sourness in place of the bitterness.

Stout: See Porter.

Wheat Beer: Wheat beer is also known by a variety of names depending on the country of origin and exact style of this ale. American wheat beers tend to be delicate and moderately hoppy, and many breweries add spices or orange peels to their wheat beer.

THE CLASSIC & CRAFT COCKTAIL RECIPE BOOK

Wine, Fortified Wine & Beer Tips

Tasting and talking about wine and beer is similar to tasting spirits once they are in the glass. First, examine the liquid. What color is it? Is there a more specific shade that it reminds you of? For beer, is it light for a stout? Is it the golden brown of an IPA? For wine, is it the bright garnet of a cabernet sauvignon or the dull ruby of a very old merlot? For wines, fortified wines, and beers, get your nose as close to the liquid as possible. Unlike whiskey, brandy, and other liquors, the alcohol content of these drams is low enough that it won't numb your nose into uselessness.

Gently swirl wine around in your glass. This motion will introduce air into the liquid, allowing it to "open up," or release flavor and scent compounds. Do not do this to beer unless you want the carbonation to dissipate; instead, just sniff it. Then, take a sip. Roll it around your mouth, and let the memories flow. Aromas and flavors can be hard to describe, but the experience will likely call up past experience of flavor and scent. Yours will be different from that of the person next to you. What you taste as strawberry may be currant to someone else, and your barnyard funk may be someone else's weird and off-putting earthiness. In the end, it is all subjective.

The debate over whether different varietals of wine need different glassware is both contentious and ongoing. Testing whether glassware makes a significant difference to the taste of the liquid inside is difficult to do. To get your home bar going, the answer is simple: Buy red wine glasses. The wider bowls may not be ideal for chilled whites, but they're a damn sight better than pouring the wine into a red plastic cup. For our purposes, fortified wines may be served in red wine glasses or cocktail glasses.

Within the beer world, the pint glass is all but eschewed as one half of a Boston shaker rather than a proper drinking vessel. As with wine, it is unclear whether the shape of the beer glass makes an appreciable difference, though beer lovers will tell you that a pilsner glass puts the beer's color on display, whereas a snifter gives the best experience of a stout's range. However, for home drinking, the pint glass is typically the best place to start.

Storing beer and wine is another contentious matter. Aging the liquid in a glass, a process known as cellaring, is much more common for wine than beer. Before cellaring a beer, consult a fellow beer snob who may have tips on which beers to cellar. Some beers improve with age, whereas others do not. Keep all cellared beverages away from light and temperature change. Like other alcoholic beverages, beer and wine will be affected, mostly negatively, by being left in direct sunlight and fluctuating temperatures. Canned beer won't survive cellaring, so drink it within three months or so of buying it. Lighter beers should be served colder; darker beers may benefit from being sipped at closer to room temperature.

If you're planning to mix cocktails with wine, fortified wine, or beer, do some research first. In modern beer cocktails, beer is often used as a finishing ingredient in place of soda or champagne. Other beer cocktails simply dress up a certain style of beer by adding hot sauce, spices, or bitters. Many of the same tenets go for wine. It is not mixed as frequently as its cousin, fortified wine, but it can add something different when mixed or used as a finishing ingredient. For all these cases, the extreme variety of beers (ranging from rich and chocolaty to bitter and citrusy to light and fruity) makes it difficult to give exact suggestions for ways to experiment with mixing it into new cocktails. The same goes with wine, although one easy tip is not to use wine that has gone unused behind your bar. If you wouldn't drink it straight, it is not going to have a positive impact on the final cocktail. In both cases, it can be said that if you're planning to experiment with a new beer or wine cocktail, drink the beer or wine by itself before mixing it at all. Doing so will give you a much better grasp of its flavor profile and may also generate ideas for complementary flavors.

CLASSIC
WINE, FORTIFIED WINE & BEER COCKTAILS

Americano BITTERSWEET
HIGHBALL GLASS | KNIFE, JIGGER

1½ ounces Campari liqueur
1½ ounces sweet vermouth
Club soda, for topping
1 orange slice or twist (see page 49), for garnish

Fill a chilled highball glass with ice. Add the Campari and vermouth, and top generously with club soda. Garnish with an orange slice or twist, and serve.

Mezzo-Mezzo: *Substitute Zucca or another rhubarb liqueur for Campari.*

Black Velvet BUBBLY
HIGHBALL GLASS | BAR SPOON

Guinness beer, to fill glass halfway
Champagne or sparkling wine, for topping

Fill a chilled highball glass halfway with beer. Pour the champagne over a spoon held near the surface of the beer until the glass is full and serve.

Michelada SAVORY

PINT GLASS | JIGGER, BAR SPOON

Salt rim (see page 49)
¾ ounce freshly squeezed lime juice
2 dashes hot sauce, preferably Valentina
1 dash Worcestershire sauce
Light-style lager beer, for topping

Pour all ingredients except the beer into a chilled, salt-rimmed pint glass, and fill halfway with ice. Top with the beer, stir gently, and serve.

Spicy Michelada: *Add a few more dashes of hot sauce.*

Shandy TART, SWEET, FIZZY

PINT GLASS

Lemonade, to fill glass halfway
Pale ale, for topping

Fill a chilled pint glass halfway with lemonade, fill the rest of the glass with beer, and serve.

Radler: *Substitute your favorite German beer for the pale ale.*
Snakebite: *Substitute lager for pale ale and hard cider for lemonade.*

Sherry Cobbler FRUITY, SWEET
COLLINS GLASS | KNIFE, JIGGER, SHAKER, MUDDLER

1 (⅛-inch-thick) orange slice
4 ounces sherry
½ tablespoon superfine sugar
1 teaspoon maraschino cherry liqueur (optional)

In a cocktail shaker, lightly muddle the orange slice. Add the remaining ingredients, shake well with cracked ice, and pour unstrained into a chilled Collins glass. Garnish with berries or any fruit you wish, and serve.

Port Cobbler: *Substitute port for sherry.*

White Wine Spritzer FRUITY, BUBBLY
RED WINE GLASS | KNIFE, JIGGER

3 ounces aromatic white wine
1 ounce club soda, for topping
1 dash orange or lemon bitters (store-bought or homemade, page 40), for topping
1 orange or lemon twist (see page 49), for garnish

Pour the wine into a chilled red wine glass filled with ice. Top with the club soda and bitters, garnish with the orange twist, and serve.

Red Wine Spritzer: *Substitute red wine for white.*
Rosé Spritzer: *Substitute rosé for white.*

WINE, FORTIFIED WINE & BEER

CRAFT
WINE, FORTIFIED WINE & BEER COCKTAILS

Adonis STRONG

COCKTAIL GLASS OR WINEGLASS | MIXING GLASS, BAR SPOON, HAWTHORNE STRAINER

1½ ounces dry oloroso sherry
1½ ounces sweet vermouth
2 dashes orange bitters (store-bought or homemade, page 40)
1 orange peel, for garnish

In a mixing glass, stir the first 3 ingredients well with ice. Strain into a chilled cocktail or wine glass, garnish with the orange peel, and serve.

Bamboo STRONG

COCKTAIL GLASS | KNIFE, JIGGER, MIXING GLASS, BAR SPOON, HAWTHORNE STRAINER

1½ ounces dry amontillado sherry
1½ ounces Noilly Prat dry vermouth
2 dashes orange bitters (store-bought or homemade, page 40)
1 dash Angostura bitters
1 twist of lemon (see page 49), for garnish

In a mixing glass, stir all liquid ingredients well with cracked ice. Strain into a chilled cocktail glass, garnish with a twist of lemon, and serve.

THE CLASSIC & CRAFT COCKTAIL RECIPE BOOK

Bicicletta STRONG
RED WINE GLASS | KNIFE, JIGGER, BAR SPOON

2 ounces Campari liqueur
2 ounces white wine, Italian and dry
Soda water, for topping
1 orange wheel (see page 49), for garnish

Pour the Campari liqueur and white wine into a chilled red wine glass. Add ice, and top with the soda. Stir gently, garnish with an orange wheel, and serve.

Bishop Cocktail STRONG
RED WINE GLASS | KNIFE, JIGGER, SHAKER, MUDDLER, HAWTHORNE STRAINER, BAR SPOON

1 lemon half wheel (see page 49), plus 1 more for garnish
1 ounce Simple Syrup (page 44)
1 ounce white rum
2 ounces red wine

In a cocktail shaker, muddle 1 lemon slice and the Simple Syrup. Add the rum and ice, and shake well. Strain into a chilled red wine glass, and add 3 ice cubes. Pour in the red wine, and stir gently to combine. Garnish with the other lemon wheel, and serve.

Black and Tan BUBBLY, STRONG
PINT GLASS

Pale ale, to fill glass halfway
Stout, to layer

Fill a chilled pint glass halfway with pale ale. Layer the stout so it floats on top, and serve.

WINE, FORTIFIED WINE & BEER

Campari Cooler BITTER, FRESH

ROCKS GLASS | JIGGER, SHAKER, HAWTHORNE STRAINER

1½ ounces Campari liqueur
1½ ounces grapefruit juice
½ ounce freshly squeezed orange juice

Shake all ingredients well with ice, strain into a chilled rocks glass full of ice, and serve.

Diplomat STRONG

COCKTAIL GLASS | JIGGER, MIXING GLASS, BAR SPOON, HAWTHORNE STRAINER

1½ ounces dry vermouth
1½ ounces sweet vermouth
1 dash maraschino cherry liqueur
1 dash Angostura bitters
1 maraschino cherry, for garnish

In a mixing glass, stir the liquid ingredients well with ice. Strain into a chilled cocktail glass, garnish with the cherry, and serve.

Frosé FRUITY, TART

ROCKS GLASSES | ICE CUBE TRAY, BLENDER

MAKES ABOUT 4½ CUPS, OR ABOUT 6 SERVINGS

1 (750-ml) bottle dry rosé
2 cups sliced strawberries, plus more for garnish (optional)
1 tablespoon sugar
¼ cup vodka
2 tablespoons grenadine (store-bought or homemade, page 45)

THE CLASSIC & CRAFT COCKTAIL RECIPE BOOK

Freeze the rosé in an ice cube tray until solid, 8 hours or overnight. In a blender, blend to combine the strawberries and sugar, and let sit for about 10 minutes at room temperature. Add the rosé ice cubes and the remaining ingredients, and blend until smooth. Pour into chilled rocks glasses, garnish with strawberries if you wish, and serve.

Port Flip CREAMY

COCKTAIL GLASS | SHAKER, HAWTHORNE STRAINER, FINE STRAINER, ZESTER OR GRATER

1 whole egg
2½ ounces port
1 teaspoon Simple Syrup (page 44)
Freshly shaved nutmeg

Crack a whole egg into a cocktail shaker, and add the port and Simple Syrup. Shake without ice, then add ice, and shake again. Double strain into a chilled cocktail glass, shave nutmeg on top, and serve.

Stout Float CREAMY, RICH

PINT GLASS | ICE CREAM SCOOP

Stout beer of choice, to fill glass two-thirds full
3 scoops vanilla ice cream
Spoon or straw

Fill a chilled pint glass two-thirds full of beer, and add the ice cream. Serve with a spoon and/or a straw.

Vermouth Spritzer FRUITY, BITTER

ROCKS GLASS | KNIFE, JIGGER

2 ounces dry or sweet vermouth
Club soda, for topping
1 orange wedge, for garnish
1 maraschino cherry, for garnish

Pour the vermouth into a chilled rocks glass full of ice. Top with the soda, garnish with the orange wedge and cherry, and serve.

Wine Granita SLUSHY, SWEET

ROCKS GLASSES | 9-BY-13-INCH METAL BAKING PAN, SPATULA

MAKES ABOUT 5½ CUPS, OR 6 SERVINGS

2 cups Honey Syrup (page 44)
1 (750-ml) bottle red wine

Chill a 9-by-13-inch metal baking pan in the freezer for 2 hours. Pour the Honey Syrup and wine into the chilled pan, stir with the spatula, and return it to the freezer. Freeze, stirring and scraping frozen parts every 30 minutes. Do not let it freeze through, but spoon it into chilled rocks glasses when it reaches the consistency of a snow cone, and serve.

THE CLASSIC & CRAFT COCKTAIL RECIPE BOOK

CHAPTER TWELVE

PUNCHES

Hundreds of years ago, most bars served communal punches instead of single serving cocktails. In that time, parties would order a bowl of punch for shared consumption. Punch brought together people from all different social strata, especially during the British navy's glory days. After the advent of the individual cocktail in the mid-1800s, punch came back into fashion for a few years in the later part of the century but then quickly went out of style.

THESE TIPPLES WERE FAR from the syrupy-sweet concoctions served in trash cans at fraternity parties. Originally, punches were much subtler and served in tiny cups so drinkers could stay and socialize for long periods rather than tapping out after a drink or two.

Finding the ingredients for punches may be difficult, but once you have them, most punches are pretty easy to make. They are also perfect for parties: Once the prep work is done, your guests will act as the bartender, meaning that the host is free to socialize and partake as well.

PUNCHES

 Champagne Punch FRUITY, BUBBLY

PUNCH GLASSES | KNIFE, JIGGER, PUNCH BOWL, LADLE

MAKES ABOUT 8 CUPS

1 (1-liter) bottle club soda, chilled
1 (750-ml) bottle brut champagne
1½ ounces brandy
1½ ounces Cointreau
Large ice block
Rind of 1 orange, for garnish
Pineapple slices, for garnish
Orange slices, for garnish
Leaves of 8 to 10 fresh mint sprigs, for garnish
Crushed strawberries for garnish (optional)

In a punch bowl, combine the first 4 ingredients and a huge block of ice. Decorate with the orange rind, sliced fresh pineapple and orange, plenty of fresh mint leaves, and strawberries (if using), and serve.

Chatham Artillery Punch HERBAL, FRUITY

PUNCH GLASSES | KNIFE, LARGE CONTAINER (NOT METAL
OR PLASTIC), PUNCH BOWL, LADLE

MAKES ABOUT 28 CUPS

2 ounces green tea leaves
4 large lemons, divided
½ pound light brown sugar
1 quart dark rum
1 quart brandy
1 quart rye whiskey
Large ice block
3 (750-ml) bottles champagne

In a quart of cold water, soak the tea leaves 8 hours or overnight. Strain the liquid from the leaves into a large container
that will hold all the spirits. Add the strained juice of 3 of the
lemons to the tea, and add the sugar, stirring until the sugar is
dissolved. Stir in the rum, brandy, and whiskey. Cover, and let
stand at room temperature for 8 hours to a week. Before serving, thinly slice the remaining lemon. Pour the mixture over a
large block of ice in the punch bowl. Swirl in the champagne,
float the sliced lemon on top, and serve.

Clarified Milk Punch CREAMY

PUNCH GLASSES | ZESTER OR GRATER, MUDDLER, LARGE CONTAINER
(NOT METAL OR PLASTIC), LARGE SAUCEPAN, FINE STRAINER,
CHEESECLOTH, PUNCH BOWL, LADLE

MAKES ABOUT 10 CUPS

Zest of 6 lemons
2 tablespoons superfine sugar
½ gallon whole milk
1⅓ cups freshly squeezed lemon juice (from about 10 lemons)
1¾ cups Demerara Syrup (page 44), plus more if needed
2 cups Cognac
1 quart demerara rum
Large ice block
Freshly grated nutmeg

Use the lemon zest and sugar to make oleo saccharum.* In a
saucepan over high heat, heat the milk, stirring constantly,
until steaming but not boiling. Remove from the heat, and add
the oleo saccharum and all remaining liquid ingredients. Stir
vigorously until it begins to separate. Strain through a fine
strainer lined with cheesecloth. When you are ready to serve,
pour the mixture over a large ice block in a punch bowl. To
adjust sweetness, add more Demerara Syrup or a bit more
lemon juice. Serve cold, topped with freshly grated nutmeg.

*To make the oleo saccharum: Put the zest in a bowl or container.
Add the sugar and muddle for 3 to 5 minutes. Cover and let sit
overnight. The peels will shrivel and the oils and syrup will form a
fragrant syrup. Strain the peels out and discard.

PUNCHES

Eggnog CREAMY, RICH
MUGS | 2 KITCHEN BOWLS, BEATER, ZESTER OR GRATER

MAKES ABOUT 12 CUPS

12 whole eggs
¾ cup superfine sugar
1 pint Cognac
½ pint dark rum
1 pint milk
½ pint heavy cream
Freshly grated nutmeg

Separate the eggs. Set aside the egg whites, but beat the yolks in a bowl steadily until they begin to lighten. Gradually add the sugar, and continue to beat until it has completely dissolved, about 2 minutes. Then, slowly pour in the 2 liquors followed by the milk and finally the cream. Clean the beaters, and in another bowl, beat the egg whites until they stand in stiff peaks. Fold the egg whites into the yolk mixture, and stir in the nutmeg. Pour into mugs, and serve.

Fish House Punch FRUITY
PUNCH GLASSES | PUNCH BOWL, LADLE

MAKES ABOUT 25 CUPS

1½ cups superfine sugar
2 quarts water
1 quart freshly squeezed lemon juice
2 quarts dark rum
1 quart Cognac
4 ounces peach brandy
Large ice block

THE CLASSIC & CRAFT COCKTAIL RECIPE BOOK

Pour the sugar into the punch bowl. Stir with enough water to dissolve it, and then stir in the lemon juice. Next, add the booze and the rest of the water (if it is summer, add a bit less). Add the ice block, and let stand, covered, in the shade for 1 hour before serving.

Pisco Punch FRUITY
PUNCH GLASSES | KNIFE, PUNCH BOWL, LADLE

MAKES ABOUT 8 CUPS

3 cups pisco brandy
1 pint distilled water
1 cup Pineapple Syrup (page 47)
10 ounces freshly squeezed lemon juice
Large ice block
Pineapple squares, for garnish

In a punch bowl, mix all liquid ingredients. Serve with a big block of ice. Serve with a soaked pineapple square in each glass.

Rum Punch CITRUSY
PUNCH GLASSES | PITCHER, ZESTER OR GRATER

MAKES ABOUT 14 CUPS

4 cups freshly squeezed orange juice
2½ cups amber rum
2 cups Simple Syrup (see page 44)
1 cup freshly squeezed lime juice
4 dashes bitters
Freshly grated nutmeg, to taste

In a pitcher, combine all liquid ingredients. Add grated nutmeg to taste, refrigerate until chilled, and serve over ice.

Sangria FRUITY, DRY

WINEGLASSES OR PUNCH GLASSES | KNIFE, PITCHER, BAR SPOON

MAKES ABOUT 6 CUPS

1 (750-ml) bottle dry red wine
¼ cup brandy
2 tablespoons granulated sugar
2 oranges, sliced
½ lemon, sliced
1 green apple, sliced
1½ cups seltzer

In a pitcher, stir together the wine, brandy, and sugar, dissolving the sugar. Add the sliced fruit, and refrigerate for at least 1 hour. Add the seltzer just before serving.

White Sangria FRUITY, DRY

WINEGLASSES OR PUNCH GLASSES | KNIFE, PITCHER, BAR SPOON

MAKES ABOUT 6 CUPS

1 (750-ml) bottle dry white wine
¼ cup white rum
2 tablespoons sugar
2 oranges, sliced
½ lemon, sliced
½ cup strawberries, sliced
1½ cups seltzer

In a pitcher, stir together the wine, rum, and sugar, dissolving the sugar. Add the sliced fruit, and refrigerate for at least 1 hour. Add the seltzer just before serving.

CHAPTER THIRTEEN

SHOOTERS

Sometimes, you want to get the party started quickly. High school reunions, family holidays—whatever the occasion, it may warrant a quick sip of straight liquor, usually called a shot, or something strong and mixed, called a shooter. Take those definitions with a grain of salt: Though generally true, the two terms may be interchangeable in some regions, or there may be other differences. All that to say, your mileage may vary.

THE RECIPES THAT FOLLOW range from well-balanced sippers to gross-out concoctions. The drink names vary from cute and slightly strange to downright sexual and offensive due to their origin in the Dark Ages of Cocktails (page 60). No matter your preference, these recipes will give you the perfect excuse to break out your collection of souvenir shot glasses.

SHOOTERS

After 5 CREAMY, PEPPERMINTY
SHOT GLASS | JIGGER

½ ounce coffee liqueur, such as Kahlúa
½ ounce peppermint schnapps
½ ounce Irish cream liqueur, such as Baileys

Pour the ingredients in the order listed into a shot glass. Drink in one swallow.

Alabama Slammer SWEET, FRUITY
SHOT GLASS | JIGGER, SHAKER, HAWTHORNE STRAINER

½ ounce Southern Comfort liqueur
½ ounce amaretto
½ ounce sloe gin
¼ ounce freshly squeezed orange juice

Shake all ingredients well with ice, and strain into a shot glass. Drink in one swallow.

B–52 CREAMY
SHOT GLASS | JIGGER

½ ounce coffee liqueur, such as Kahlúa
½ ounce Irish cream liqueur, such as Baileys
½ ounce Triple Sec or Grand Marnier

Layer the three spirits in the order listed into a shot glass. Drink in one swallow.

Bloody Mary Shot STRONG, SAVORY

SHOT GLASS | PITCHER

MAKES 10 SHOTS

½ cup vodka
9 ounces tomato juice
1 ounce lemon juice
3 dashes hot sauce, preferably Tabasco
½ tablespoon Worcestershire sauce
1 teaspoon celery salt
Tiny celery stalks, for garnish
½ teaspoon freshly ground black pepper, for garnish

Combine all liquid ingredients and celery salt in a pitcher, and stir. Pour into shot glasses and garnish with the tiny celery sticks and a pinch of black pepper.

Blowjob CREAMY

SHOT GLASS | JIGGER

¼ ounce Irish cream liqueur, such as Baileys
½ ounce amaretto liqueur
Whipped cream, for topping

Pour both liqueurs into a shot glass, and top with whipped cream. Traditionally the drinker places their hands behind their back and picks up the shot glass with their mouth, tilts their head back, and drinks.

Boilermaker STRONG
SHOT GLASS, PINT GLASS | JIGGER

1½ ounces whiskey
Beer of your choice, for chasing

Serve the whiskey in a shot glass next to the beer.

Breakfast Shot SWEET
2 SHOT GLASSES | JIGGER

1 ounce Irish whiskey
½ ounce butterscotch schnapps
Freshly squeezed orange juice, for chasing

Pour the whiskey and schnapps in one shot glass. Pour orange juice into the second shot glass. Drink the first shot in one swallow, and chase with the orange juice.

Buttery Nipple SWEET, CREAMY
SHOT GLASS | JIGGER

½ ounce vodka
½ ounce Irish cream liqueur, such as Baileys
½ ounce butterscotch schnapps

Pour all ingredients into a shot glass, and drink in one gulp.

Cement Mixer GROSS
SHOT GLASS | JIGGER

1 ounce Irish cream liqueur, such as Baileys
½ ounce freshly squeezed lime juice

Pour both ingredients into a shot glass. When they curdle, drink in one gulp.

Chip Shot CREAMY, COFFEE
SMALL ROCKS GLASS | JIGGER

1 ounce citrus liqueur, such as Tuaca
1 ounce Irish cream liqueur, such as Baileys
1 ounce hot coffee

Pour the citrus liqueur and Irish cream liqueur into a small rocks glass. Splash the hot coffee on top, and serve.

Chocolate Cake SWEET, CHOCOLATEY
SHOT GLASS | KNIFE, JIGGER

1 ounce hazelnut liqueur, such as Frangelico
½ ounce vodka
1 sugared lemon slice (see page 49)

Combine the hazelnut liqueur and vodka in a shot glass. Suck the lemon wedge, and with the juice still in your mouth, drink the shot in one swallow.

Cordless Screwdriver CITRUSY
SHOT GLASS | KNIFE, JIGGER, SHAKER, HAWTHORNE STRAINER

1 ounce vodka
1 sugared orange slice (see page 49)

Shake the vodka with ice, and strain into a shot glass. Shoot the vodka, and eat the orange.

Flaming Doctor Pepper Shot SWEET

PINT GLASS, SHOT GLASS

¾ shot amaretto liqueur
About ¼ ounce 151 proof rum
½ glass beer

Fill a shot glass about three-quarters full with amaretto, and float enough 151 on top to light on fire, about ¼ ounce. Place the shot glass in the pint glass, and fill the outer glass with beer up to the brim of the shot glass. Ignite the 151, and let it burn for a minute or two. Blow it out, and drink it quickly.

French Kiss SWEET, CREAMY

SHOT GLASS | JIGGER

½ ounce amaretto liqueur
½ ounce crème de cacao
½ ounce Irish cream liqueur, such as Baileys

Layer the ingredients into a shot glass in the order listed. Drink in one swallow.

Girl Scout Cookie Shot

CHOCOLATEY, PEPPERMINTY, SWEET

SHOT GLASS | JIGGER, SHAKER, HAWTHORNE STRAINER

½ ounce Irish cream liqueur, such as Baileys
½ ounce coffee liqueur, such as Kahlúa
½ ounce peppermint schnapps

Shake all 3 ingredients, strain into a shot glass, and drink in one swallow.

Green Lizard STRONG

SHOT GLASS | JIGGER

1 ounce 151 proof rum
1 ounce green Chartreuse

Combine the rum and green Chartreuse in a shot glass, and drink in one swallow.

Harbor Lights CITRUSY, COFFEE

CORDIAL GLASS | JIGGER, TEASPOON

½ ounce coffee liqueur, such as Kahlúa
½ ounce Triple Sec
½ ounce Cognac
1 teaspoon 151 white rum

Pour the coffee liqueur, Triple Sec, and Cognac into a cordial glass. Ignite the rum in a teaspoon, and float on top. Extinguish, and serve.

Irish Car Bomb CREAMY, STRONG

PINT GLASS, SHOT GLASS | JIGGER

½ ounce Irish cream liqueur, such as Baileys
½ ounce Irish whiskey, such as Jameson
½ pint Guinness beer

Pour the Irish cream liqueur and Irish whiskey into a shot glass. Drop the shot (glass and all) into ½ pint of Guinness beer, and drink it quickly.

Jäger Bomb STRONG
HIGHBALL GLASS, SHOT GLASS

½ can energy drink, preferably Red Bull
1½ ounces Jägermeister liqueur

Pour the energy drink into a highball glass. Drop in a shot glass of Jägermeister, and drink the foaming concoction as quickly as possible.

Jelly Bean ANISE, CANDY
ROCKS GLASS | JIGGER, SHAKER, HAWTHORNE STRAINER

1 ounce blackberry brandy
1 ounce anisette

Shake both ingredients well with ice, and strain into a rocks glass. Drink in one swallow.

Kamikaze CITRUSY, SWEET
SHOT GLASS | JIGGER, SHAKER, HAWTHORNE STRAINER

1 ounce vodka
½ ounce Triple Sec
½ ounce freshly squeezed lime juice

Shake all ingredients well with ice, strain into a shot glass, and drink in one swallow.

Key Lime Pie CITRUSY, CREAMY

SHOT GLASS | JIGGER, SHAKER, HAWTHORNE STRAINER

1 ounce vodka
¾ ounce lime cordial, such as Rose's
½ ounce cream
¼ ounce sweet-and-sour mix

Shake all ingredients well with ice, strain into a shot glass, and drink in one swallow.

Lemon Drop Shot CITRUSY

SHOT GLASS | JIGGER

1½ ounces citron vodka
1 sugared lemon wedge (see page 49)

Pour the vodka into a shot glass. Drink the vodka in one swallow, and bite into the lemon wedge.

Liquid Cocaine HERBAL, SWEET

SHOT GLASS | JIGGER, SHAKER, HAWTHORNE STRAINER

½ ounce 151 proof rum
½ ounce Rumple Minze
½ ounce Jägermeister liqueur
½ ounce Goldschläger

Shake all ingredients well with ice, strain into a shot glass, and drink in one swallow.

Melon Ball *FRUITY, SWEET*

SHOT GLASS | JIGGER, SHAKER, HAWTHORNE STRAINER

½ ounce vodka
½ ounce melon liqueur (preferably Midori)
½ ounce pineapple juice

Shake all ingredients well with ice, and strain into a shot glass. Drink in one swallow.

Mind Eraser *COFFEE*

SHOT GLASS | JIGGER

½ ounce coffee liqueur, such as Kahlúa
½ ounce vodka
Soda, for topping

Pour into a shot glass in the order listed, and drink in one swallow.

Nutty Irishman *CREAMY, SWEET*

SHOT GLASS | JIGGER, SHAKER, HAWTHORNE STRAINER

½ ounce Irish cream liqueur, such as Baileys Irish cream
½ ounce hazelnut liqueur, such as Frangelico
½ ounce cream

Shake all ingredients well with ice, strain into a shot glass, and drink in one swallow.

Oatmeal Cookie Shot SWEET, CINNAMON

SHOT GLASS | JIGGER

½ ounce cinnamon schnapps
½ ounce butterscotch schnapps
½ ounce Irish cream liqueur, such as Baileys Irish cream

Layer all ingredients into a shot glass in the order listed, and drink in one swallow.

PB&J Shot FRUITY, NUTTY

SHOT GLASS | JIGGER, SHAKER, HAWTHORNE STRAINER

¾ ounce hazelnut liqueur, such as Frangelico
¾ ounce raspberry liqueur, such as Chambord

Shake both ingredients well with ice, strain into a shot glass, and drink in one swallow.

Prairie Fire SPICY, STRONG

SHOT GLASS | JIGGER

3 or 4 dashes Tabasco
1½ ounces tequila

Dash the Tabasco into a shot glass, and add the tequila. Drink in one swallow.

Purple Hooter SWEET, FRUITY

SHOT GLASS | JIGGER, SHAKER, HAWTHORNE STRAINER

½ ounce vodka
½ ounce raspberry liqueur, such as Chambord
Lemon-lime soda, for topping

Shake the vodka and raspberry liqueur well with ice. Strain into a shot glass, top with lemon-lime soda, and drink in one swallow.

Red–Headed Slut SWEET, FRUITY
SHOT GLASS | JIGGER, BAR SPOON

½ ounce Jägermeister liqueur
½ ounce peach schnapps
Cranberry juice, for topping

Pour the alcohol into a shot glass, fill with cranberry juice, and stir to mix. Drink in one swallow.

Red Snapper SWEET, FRUITY
SHOT GLASS | JIGGER, MIXING GLASS, BAR SPOON, HAWTHORNE STRAINER

1 ounce Canadian whisky, such as Crown Royal
½ ounce amaretto liqueur
1 splash cranberry juice

In a mixing glass, stir all ingredients well with ice. Strain into a shot glass, and drink in one swallow.

Russian Quaalude NUTTY, CREAMY
SHOT GLASS | JIGGER, SHAKER, HAWTHORNE STRAINER

½ ounce vodka
½ ounce coffee liqueur, such as Kahlúa
½ ounce Irish cream liqueur, such as Baileys
½ ounce hazelnut liqueur, such as Frangelico

Shake all ingredients well with ice, and strain into a shot glass. Drink in one swallow.

Screaming Orgasm Shot FRUITY
SHOT GLASS | JIGGER, SHAKER, HAWTHORNE STRAINER

¼ ounce vodka
¼ ounce amaretto liqueur
¼ ounce coffee liqueur
¼ ounce Irish cream liqueur, such as Baileys

Shake all ingredients well with ice, and strain into a shot glass. Drink in one swallow.

Sex on the Beach Shot FRUITY, SWEET
SHOT GLASS | JIGGER, SHAKER, HAWTHORNE STRAINER

¾ ounce vodka
¾ ounce peach schnapps
¾ ounce freshly squeezed orange juice

Shake all ingredients well with ice, and strain into a shot glass. Drink in one swallow.

Snakebite STRONG, SPICY
SHOT GLASS | JIGGER

1 dash Tabasco
¾ ounce Tennessee whisky, such as Jack Daniel's
¾ ounce tequila

Dash the Tabasco into a shot glass. Add the remaining ingredients, and drink in one swallow.

THE CLASSIC & CRAFT COCKTAIL RECIPE BOOK

Surfer on Acid Shooter TROPICAL, SWEET, FRUITY

SHOT GLASS | JIGGER, SHAKER, HAWTHORNE STRAINER

¾ ounce Jägermeister liqueur
½ ounce coconut rum
½ ounce pineapple juice

Shake all ingredients well with ice, and strain into a shot glass. Drink in one swallow.

Terminator SWEET

SHOT GLASS | JIGGER, SHAKER, HAWTHORNE STRAINER

1 ounce Jägermeister liqueur
1 ounce Southern Comfort liqueur

Shake both ingredients well with ice, and strain into a shot glass. Drink in one swallow.

Washington Apple FRUITY, SWEET

SHOT GLASS | JIGGER, SHAKER, HAWTHORNE STRAINER

½ ounce Canadian whisky, such as Crown Royal
½ ounce sour apple schnapps
½ ounce cranberry juice
1 splash lemon-lime soda (optional)

Shake the first 3 ingredients, and strain into a shot glass. Add a splash of soda, if desired, and serve.

Woo Woo FRUITY, SWEET
SHOT GLASS | KNIFE, JIGGER, SHAKER, HAWTHORNE STRAINER

½ ounce vodka
½ ounce peach schnapps
½ ounce cranberry juice
1 lime wedge, for garnish

Shake all liquid ingredients well with ice. Strain into a
chilled shot glass, garnish with a lime wedge, and drink in
one swallow.

THE CLASSIC & CRAFT COCKTAIL RECIPE BOOK

CHAPTER FOURTEEN

HOT BEVERAGES

On a cold winter day, few things are quite as satisfying as a hot cocktail. In the time before central heating, these beverages might have been one of the only ways to fortify your body against the cold. It is not surprising that some of these recipes are centuries old. Over time, the original recipes have been lost or adapted based on what ingredients were locally available. Though heating the drinks would have been a larger challenge then, the biggest challenge now is deciding which one to drink first.

WHEN YOU START MAKING THESE DRINKS, remember not to boil alcoholic ingredients: The process can negatively change their flavor and their alcohol content. Also, remember that heat intensifies the smell of alcohol. To avoid a face full of alcohol fumes, serve finished drinks in a pre-warmed mug or another glass with a wide mouth. This approach comes with an added bonus: Just as chilling glasses for cold cocktails helps keep them at temperature, so too will pre-warmed cups keep hot beverages at temperature.

When you begin testing your own recipes, go light on bitter and sour ingredients: Heat intensifies negative aspects of both of these flavors. Heat also decreases the perception of sweetness, so add a bit more honey or sugar than you usually would.

HOT BEVERAGES

Apple Toddy APPLEY
MUGS | BAKING SHEET, KNIFE, MUDDLER, ZESTER OR GRATER

MAKES 2 SERVINGS

1 apple, peeled and cored
2 tablespoons maple syrup or sweetener of choice, divided
About 4 ounces boiling water, divided
4 ounces apple brandy, divided
Fresh grated nutmeg, for garnish

Preheat the oven to 350 degrees Fahrenheit. Wrap the apple
in parchment paper, and place it on a baking sheet. Bake for
30 to 45 minutes, until very soft. Rinse 2 mugs with hot water
to warm, dry, and then add 1 tablespoon syrup to each. Add a
splash of boiling water to each, and stir until the sweetener
is dissolved. Add 2 ounces of apple brandy to each mug. Cut
the apple in half and muddle one half in each mug. Add 1 to
2 ounces of boiling water to each mug, and stir until the apple
has disintegrated. Grate nutmeg over the top, and serve.

Bishop FRUITY, TART
MUGS | CERAMIC OR GLASS BAKING DISH, KNIFE, 2-QUART SAUCEPAN

MAKES ABOUT 4 SERVINGS

1 navel orange
8 whole cloves
1 (750-ml) bottle ruby port

Preheat the oven to 400 degrees Fahrenheit. Stud the orange with the cloves, and roast in the baking dish on the oven's middle rack until browned and soft, about 1½ hours. Quarter the orange, and combine the orange quarters and port in the saucepan over medium heat. Bring just barely to a simmer, and remove from the heat. Rinse mugs with hot water to warm. Dry the mugs, pour the liquid into them, and serve.

Bourbon Hot Chocolate CREAMY, SWEET
MUG | JIGGER

2 ounces bourbon
6 ounces hot chocolate
Whipped cream, for topping

Rinse a mug with hot water to warm. Dry, and pour in the bourbon and hot chocolate, top with whipped cream, and serve.

Brandy Toddy CITRUSY
MUG | JIGGER

1½ ounces brandy
1 tablespoon honey
2 teaspoons freshly squeezed lemon juice
1 cup hot water

Rinse a mug with hot water to warm. Dry, and combine the brandy, honey, and lemon juice in the mug. Top with the hot water, stir until the honey is dissolved, and serve.

THE CLASSIC & CRAFT COCKTAIL RECIPE BOOK

Café Amaretto SWEET, COFFEE

MUG | JIGGER

1½ ounces amaretto
½ ounce brandy
4 to 6 ounces hot coffee
Whipped cream, for topping

Rinse a mug with hot water to warm. Dry, and combine the amaretto and brandy in the mug. Fill with coffee, top with whipped cream, and serve.

Café Royale COFFEE

MUG | JIGGER

4 ounces hot coffee
1½ ounces brandy
1 sugar cube

Rinse a mug with hot water to warm, dry, and pour in the coffee. Combine the brandy and sugar cube in a spoon or jigger over the coffee, and set the brandy on fire. Once the fire dies down, pour into the coffee, and serve.

Hot Buttered Rum RICH, SWEET

MUG | JIGGER

2 sugar cubes
Hot water
2 ounces dark rum
Pat unsalted butter
Ground nutmeg (optional)

Rinse a mug with hot water to warm. Dry, dissolve the sugar in a bit of hot water in the mug, and then add the rum and butter. Fill the mug with hot water, sprinkle a little nutmeg on top, and serve.

Hot Toddy CITRUSY
MUG | JIGGER

1½ ounces bourbon
1 tablespoon honey
2 teaspoons freshly squeezed lemon juice
1 cup hot water

Rinse a mug with hot water to warm. Dry, and combine the bourbon, honey, and lemon juice in the mug. Top with hot water, stir until the honey is dissolved, and serve.

Irish Coffee COFFEE, CREAMY
MUG | JIGGER, BAR SPOON

2 teaspoons brown sugar
2 ounces whiskey
5 to 6 ounces coffee
Boiling water
Lightly whipped cream or heavy cream, for topping

Rinse a mug with hot water to warm. Dry, add the sugar and whiskey to the mug with about an inch of coffee, and stir to combine. Fill with coffee up to about 1 inch below the rim. Top with a thick layer of lightly whipped cream, or pour the cream over the back of a spoon, and serve.

THE CLASSIC & CRAFT COCKTAIL RECIPE BOOK

Jamaican Coffee COFFEE, STRONG

MUG | JIGGER

2 ounces rum
4 to 6 ounces hot coffee
Whipped cream, for topping

Rinse a mug with hot water to warm. Dry, add the rum, and fill
with coffee. Top with whipped cream, and serve.

Mexican Coffee COFFEE, STRONG

MUG | JIGGER

1½ ounces tequila
4 to 6 ounces hot coffee
Whipped cream, for topping

Rinse a mug with hot water to warm. Dry, add the tequila, and
fill with coffee. Top with whipped cream, and serve.

Mulled Cider APPLEY

WARM MUGS | KNIFE, LARGE SAUCEPAN WITH LID, FINE STRAINER,
HEAT-PROOF PUNCH BOWL

MAKES ABOUT 16 CUPS

1 gallon apple cider
4 cinnamon sticks, plus more for garnish
1½ teaspoons whole allspice berries
1 teaspoon whole cloves
1 navel orange, peeled and sliced
1 lemon, peeled and sliced
1 cup rum

In a large saucepan over high heat, heat the cider with the
spices and citrus slices to boiling. Reduce the heat to low.

Cover, and simmer for about 45 minutes. Add the rum, and heat through, but do not boil. Strain the cider through a fine strainer into a heatproof punch bowl. Rinse the mugs with hot water to warm. Dry the mugs, discard the used spices, and serve the cider in the warm mugs garnished with cinnamon sticks.

Mulled Wine APPLEY, FRUITY

MUGS | KNIFE, ZESTER OR GRATER, LARGE SAUCEPAN

MAKES ABOUT 8 CUPS

4 cups apple cider
1 (750-ml) bottle red wine, such as cabernet sauvignon
¼ cup honey
2 cinnamon sticks
1 orange, zested and juiced, plus peels of 4 oranges, for garnish
4 whole cloves
3 star anise pods

In a large saucepan over high heat, bring all ingredients except the orange peels to a boil. Turn the heat to low and simmer for 10 minutes. Rinse mugs with hot water to warm. Dry, pour in the wine, garnish each with an orange peel, and serve.

Peppermint Patty Hot Chocolate

MINTY, CREAMY, CHOCOLATEY
MUG | JIGGER, ZESTER OR GRATER

1 ounce peppermint schnapps
½ ounce dark crème de cacao
1 teaspoon crème de menthe
6 ounces hot chocolate
Whipped cream, for topping
Shaved chocolate, for garnish

Rinse a mug with hot water to warm. Dry, pour the liqueurs into the mug, and fill with hot chocolate. Top with whipped cream, garnish with shaved chocolate, and serve.

Rum Toddy CITRUSY
MUG | JIGGER

1½ ounces rum
1 tablespoon honey
2 teaspoons freshly squeezed lemon juice
1 cup hot water

Rinse a mug with hot water to warm. Dry, and combine the rum, honey, and lemon juice in the mug. Top with hot water, stir until the honey is dissolved, and serve.

Spicy Aztec Hot Chocolate
SPICY, CHOCOLATEY, CREAMY
MUG | KNIFE, JIGGER, SAUCEPAN, WHISK

4 cups whole milk
1 (3.2-ounce) disk Mexican chocolate, chopped
1 dried chile, stemmed, seeded, and deveined
1 cinnamon stick
1 vanilla bean
3 ounces tequila
Whipped cream, for topping

In a saucepan over medium-high heat, bring the milk to a simmer. Add the chocolate, chili, cinnamon stick, and vanilla bean, and reduce the heat to medium-low. Simmer for 10 minutes, whisking constantly. Once the chocolate is melted, remove and discard the solid ingredients. Rinse a mug with hot water to warm. Dry, pour the liquid into the heated mug, and add the tequila. Top with whipped cream and serve.

Tom and Jerry CREAMY, RICH

SMALL COFFEE MUG OR VINTAGE TOM AND JERRY MUG |
JIGGER, 2 BOWLS (NOT METAL OR PLASTIC), WHISK OR BEATER,
ZESTER OR GRATER

1 tablespoon Tom and Jerry batter (see below)
1 ounce Cognac
1 ounce dark rum
Hot whole milk, to fill
Freshly grated nutmeg, for garnish
Ground cloves, for garnish
Ground allspice, for garnish

Rinse a small coffee mug with hot water to warm. Dry, add
the batter, Cognac, and rum to the cup, and fill with hot milk.
Garnish with a sprinkle of 2 parts freshly grated nutmeg to
1 part each ground clove and ground allspice, and serve. These
are great to make for a group so you can use all your batter.

Tom and Jerry Batter

12 eggs, separated
1 teaspoon cream of tartar
2 pounds sugar
2 ounces Jamaican-style rum
1 teaspoon vanilla extract (optional)

In a bowl, whip the egg whites with the cream of tartar until
they form stiff peaks. In a separate bowl, beat the yolks with
the sugar, rum, and vanilla (if using). When the yolk mixture is
completely liquid, fold it into the whites.

THE CLASSIC & CRAFT COCKTAIL RECIPE BOOK

Wassail STRONG, FRUITY

MUGS | CHEESECLOTH, KITCHEN STRING, LARGE POT, JIGGER,
ZESTER OR GRATER

MAKES ABOUT 19 CUPS

12 whole cloves
6 whole allspice berries
½ inch fresh ginger root, peeled and sliced
3 cinnamon sticks, plus 1 cinnamon stick per drink, for garnish
12 whole white peppercorns
1 gallon fresh apple cider
6 ounces cranberry juice
¾ cup light brown sugar, packed
10 to 12 ounces bourbon
Freshly grated nutmeg, for garnish

Wrap the cloves, allspice, ginger, 3 cinnamon sticks, and peppercorns in cheesecloth, and tie with kitchen string. Combine the cider, cranberry juice, brown sugar, and spice bag in a large pot over high heat. Bring to a boil, reduce the heat, and simmer for 30 minutes. Rinse the mugs with hot water to warm. Dry, pour 1 ounce of bourbon into each, and fill with the hot cider mixture. Garnish each with a bit of nutmeg and a cinnamon stick, and serve.

Whiskey Skin STRONG
MUG OR HEATPROOF CUP | KNIFE, JIGGER, BAR SPOON

1 teaspoon demerara sugar

1 thin-cut lemon peel

2 ounces boiling water, divided

2 ounces Scotch

Rinse a mug or heatproof cup with hot water to warm. Dry, and add the sugar and a swatch of thin-cut lemon peel. Add 1 ounce boiling water, stir to dissolve the sugar, and add the Scotch. Finish by adding 1 ounce more of boiling water to heat the drink again, and serve.

THE CLASSIC & CRAFT COCKTAIL RECIPE BOOK

Further Reading

Arnold, Dave. *Liquid Intelligence: The Art and Science of the Perfect Cocktail*. New York: W. W. Norton & Co., 2014.

Berry, Jeff "Beachbum." *Beachbum Berry's Potions of the Caribbean*. New York: Cocktail Kingdom, 2013.

Berry, Jeff "Beachbum." *Beachbum Berry Remixed*. San Jose, CA: SLG Publishing, 2009.

Berry, Jeff "Beachbum." *Beachbum Berry's Sippin' Safari*. San Jose, CA: SLG Publishing, 2007.

Clarke, Paul. *The Cocktail Chronicles: Navigating the Cocktail Renaissance with Jigger, Shaker & Glass*. Nashville: Spring House Press, 2015.

Conigliaro, Tony. *The Cocktail Lab: Unraveling the Mysteries of Flavor and Aroma in Drink, with Recipes*. Berkeley, CA: Ten Speed Press, 2013.

Craddock, Henry. *The Savoy Cocktail Book*. London: Pavilion Books, 1930.

Curtis, Wayne. *And a Bottle of Rum: A History of the New World in Ten Cocktails*. New York: Broadway Books, 2007.

de Kergommeaux, Davin. *Canadian Whisky: The Portable Expert*. Toronto: McClelland & Stewart, 2012.

Dietsch, Michael. *Shrubs: An Old-Fashioned Drink for Modern Times*. Taftsville, VT: The Countryman Press, 2014.

Embury, David. *The Fine Art of Mixing Drinks*. New York: Mud Puddle Books, 1948.

Haigh, Ted. *Vintage Spirits and Forgotten Cocktails: From the Alamagoozlum to the Zombie; 100 Rediscovered Recipes and the Stories behind Them*. London: Quarry Books, 2009 reissue.

Kaplan, David, Alex Day, and Nick Fauchald. *Death & Co: Modern Classic Cocktails*. Berkeley, CA: Ten Speed Press, 2014.

MacNeil, Karen. *The Wine Bible*. New York: Workman Publishing, 2000.

Meehan, Jim. *The PDT Cocktail Book: The Complete Bartender's Guide from the Celebrated Speakeasy*. New York: Sterling Epicure, 2011.

Morgenthaler, Jeffrey. *The Bar Book: Elements of Cocktail Technique*. San Francisco: Chronicle Books, 2014.

Parson, Brad Thomas. *Bitters: A Spirited History of a Classic Cure-All with Cocktails, Recipes, and Formulas*. Berkeley, CA: Ten Speed Press, 2011.

Society of Wine Educators. *Certified Specialist of Spirits Study Guide*, 2015.

Thomas, Jerry. *How to Mix Drinks or The Bon Vivant's Companion*, 1862.

Uyeda, Kazuo. *Cocktail Techniques*. Toyko: Mud Puddle Books, 2010, English-language edition.

Wondrich, David. *Imbibe! From Absinthe Cocktail to Whiskey Smash, a Salute in Stories and Drinks to "Professor" Jerry Thomas, Pioneer of the American Bar*. New York: Perigee, 2007.

Wondrich, David. *Punch: The Delights (and Dangers) of the Flowing Bowl*. New York: Perigee, 2010.

FURTHER READING

Acknowledgments

Hey, Mom and Dad, I wrote a book! Y'all always told me that I could do anything, but I have to admit that I have not always believed it myself. This book has been a whirlwind, to be sure, but you have always believed in me, and I love you.

Endless gratitude to my husband, Adam Evans. Without you, I would not have had the chutzpah or support to quit my office job to take the bartending job, or to quit the bartending gig to write. I love you.

Huge thanks also to Sara Glassman, Haley Herfurth, Laura Foster, and all of the other amazing people without whose words of encouragement this book would not have been possible. Big, big thanks to Nathan and Brooke McMinn, Alan Kennedy, Brad Culverhouse, Gia Bivens Atkinson, and Jen Gregory for answering my endless questions about spirits for this book. Thanks for the opportunity from the amazing team at Rockridge Press.

Lastly, thanks to Feast & Forest, Marty's PM, and Dave's Pub for letting me celebrate deadlines or slack off for a few minutes. Your sustenance and support got me through this process, and I will not forget that quickly.

Recipe Index

RECIPE INDEX

RECIPE INDEX

W

Y

Z

Index

About the Author

Clair McLafferty is a freelance writer, teacher, and bartender-at-large based in Birmingham, Alabama. When she is not researching or writing about cocktails, Clair is probably nerding out on trashy science fiction or snuggling with her husband and two dogs. She has many favorite cocktails but will usually order a pour of whiskey neat, especially during a gathering of the Birmingham Bourbon Club. Her other writing and rambling is usually posted on Twitter @see_clair_write and at clairmclafferty.com.

CPSIA information can be obtained
at www.ICGtesting.com
Printed in the USA
BVHW062353251119
564756BV00024B/616/P

9 781623 158477